KISS
HOTTER THAN HELL

KISS

HOTTER THAN HELL

THE STORIES BEHIND EVERY SONG

PAUL ELLIOTT

METRO BOOKS
NEW YORK

This 2009 edition published by Metro Books,
by arrangement with Carlton Books Limited

PROJECT EDITOR: Lorna Russell

PICTURE RESEARCH: Adrian Bentley

DESIGNER: Brian Flynn

ART EDITOR: Vicky Holmes

COVER DESIGN: Alison Tutton

PRODUCTION: Janette Davis

Metro Books
122 Fifth Avenue
New York, NY 10011

ISBN: 978-1-4351-1537-8

10 9 8 7 6 5 4 3 2 1

Printed and bound in Dubai

The publishers would like to thank the following sources for their kind permission to reproduce the pictures in this book:

ALL ACTION: /Harry Goodwin: 66; /Suzan Moore: 36-37, 40, 43, 54, 68, 86tc, 91, 97, 103, 142, 144; /Duncan Raban:
118tr; /Justin Thomas: 27, 33, 41, 78, 127, 130, 133, 136-137.
KARL BRADLEY: 26.
REDFERNS: /George Chin: 135; /Fin Costello: 15, 70, 76, 89, 94, 98-99; /Ian Dickson: 109, /Gems: 88; /Glenn A. Baker
Archive: 111; /Robert Knight: 74; /Michael Ochs Archives: 45, 73, 84; /Steve Morley: 6-7, 77; /Ebet Roberts: 48, 90;
/S & G Press Agency: 100.
REX FEATURES: 12, 55, 56-57, 59, 64, 80-81, 116, 117, 122, 132, 141; /Eugene Adebari: 24, 87, 104, 107, 112; /A. di
Crollalanza: 52; /Fotos International/M. E. Marzouk: 75; /Karen Fuchs: 93; /Harry Goodwin: 65bc, 86br; /Nils
Jorgensen: 19bl, 110; /Media Press International: 60-61, 69; /Erik Pendzich: 28; /Brian Rasic: 8, 17, 62; /Sipa: 20-21;
/Sipa/Ed Carreon: 19tr; /Laurens van Houten: 115; /A. Vereecke: 118bl; /Richard Young: 10-11.
S.I.N.: /Alessio: 23; /Peter Anderson: 71, 113, 131; /Richard Beland: 51; /Karena Bernard: 128; /David Corio: 65tr, 129;
/Martyn Goodacre: 63; /Jayne Houghton: 123; /Don Lewis: 58; /K. Natola: 30, 46; /Phil Regendanz: 120; /Ian T. Tilton:
124, 126.

Every effort has been made to acknowledge correctly and contact the source and/or copyright holder of each picture,
and Carlton Books Limited apologises for any unintentional errors or omissions which will be corrected in future
editions of this book

CONTENTS

INTRODUCTION

"You wanted the best and you got the best – the hottest band in the world, Kiss!"

For three decades, Kiss have delivered the ultimate rock 'n' roll spectacle. Four heavy metal superheroes in facepaint and stack heels: Paul Stanley, the pouting Starchild; Ace Frehley, the outlandish Space Ace; Peter Criss, the lovable Catman; and Gene Simmons, the fire-breathing, blood-dribbling Demon.

Kiss concerts have amazed and astounded generations of rock fans. Stanley is the ultimate rock 'n' roll showman, utterly in love with himself and straining every sinew to please his audience. Criss, famously dubbed "one of the world's foremost two-fisted tom-tom men", performs drum solos amid fireworks on a platform thirty feet above the stage. Frehley claims to be from another planet – Jendell – and plays a guitar that bursts into smoke and flames in his hands. And Simmons, the God Of Thunder, exudes a truly menacing persona as he stalks the stage before flying up to the rafters to deliver his bloody bass solo.

On top of all this, Kiss have created some of rock's greatest anthems: "Rock And Roll All Nite", "God Of Thunder", "Shout It Out Loud", "Cold Gin", plus the disco classic "I Was Made For Lovin' You" and the definitive rock ballad "Beth". As Gene Simmons declares: "How much crack would we have to be on to call ourselves 'The Hottest Band In The World' if we weren't gonna go out there and deliver?"

Derided as a mere circus act by critics, yet adored by such modern rock icons as Marilyn Manson, Nirvana and Nine Inch Nails, Kiss are a genuine American legend.

Yet their origins are humble. All four original members were raised in New York City where the band formed in 1973 from the ashes of Simmons and Stanley's group Wicked Lester. Peter Criss came from a tough Italian neighbourhood. Ace Frehley passed his Kiss

audition wearing two different-coloured sneakers. Together they formed the most over-the-top band in rock history. Wearing full face make-up, they created a mystique unrivalled in rock 'n' roll. Throughout the 1970s, Kiss were never photographed out of make-up. They seemed superhuman, like fantasy heroes from a Marvel comic. By the mid 70s, Kiss were the biggest band in America.

When Frehley and Criss departed at the turn of the 80s, Kiss rolled on. Even when they shocked fans by unmasking in 1983, Kiss remained one of the biggest bands in rock. And when drummer Eric Carr fell victim to cancer in

1991, Kiss did not falter. In 1996, the original line-up of Kiss reunited for a record-breaking world tour. Their place in the pantheon of legendary rock 'n' roll bands was assured. In America, only The Beatles have achieved more gold records.

Kiss also enjoy a truly unique relationship with their fans. This is the essence of this book. The Kiss Army fan club is famous around the world. Its members are truly fanatical in their love of the band, buying up every new item of merchandise stamped with the Kiss brand, from lunchboxes and t-shirts to Kiss cars and coffins!

Here, the fans speak out, revealing all about their obsession with Kiss and explaining why individual Kiss songs mean so much to them. The author wishes to thank these fans for their involvement in this book: Joe Mackett, Howard Johnson, Andy Hunns, Graham Stroud, Leigh Marklew, Dave Reynolds, Chris Dale, Tony Cooke, Dante Bonutto, Gary Banton, Mark Taylor and Rudy Reed.

As Gene Simmons states: "Kiss is of the people, for the people."

It is to the people listed above, and to Kiss fans everywhere, that this book is dedicated.

Rock and roll all nite. And party every day.

Paul Elliott, Brighton, England, May 2002

"We wound up playing together because we had a shared vision and philosophy. Although we're totally different as people, the core, the work ethic, is very much the same."

1

PAUL STANLEY & GENE SIMMONS
founder members of Kiss,
in conversation with author Paul Elliott.

For more than three decades, Paul Stanley and Gene Simmons have led the most outrageous rock 'n' roll band on the planet. Here, they talk candidly about Kiss: the band's early days in New York City; their first meeting in the early 1970s; their legendary live performances; how they coped with superstar fame, their attitudes to the rock 'n' roll lifestyle of sex and booze and drugs; their lack of critical acclaim; and their reputation as "The Hottest Band In The World".

How poor were you when Kiss were just starting out in New York City during the early 1970s?
Paul: "Nothing seems desperate when you don't think it's permanent. We always had this attitude and that, boy, we're gonna look back on this fondly. When we were in a cold loft in New York, rehearsing and drinking sherry to keep warm, we thought, Well, this is the kind of stuff that books are made of. These are the days we'll look back on and say, 'Remember the good old days?'. So we never had any real tough times. Everything we went through seemed to us like another part of the Kiss story, like we were living this movie. We were the stars of our own film.

"We were lucky, because all of us were living at home. My parents were trying to kick me out, they thought it was about time I got a job. We weren't starving, we were just scraping by to pay for rehearsal space. At one point I became a cab driver. I would drive my taxi to rehearsal, drop the gear, do the rehearsal and then go back in the cab and go back to work. It was great. There were no terrible times."

Did you ever have anybody famous in your cab?
Paul: "No. You hear all these great cab stories, but the funniest thing that happened to me was I was

driving and this guy was sitting in the back seat and I was thinking, 'My God, this guy is famous, he's a big actor, I just can't place where I've seen him but I know his face, he's a very famous person.' For weeks it was going through my head.

"My parents lived in a two-floor apartment building and there I was sitting in the window one afternoon, taking it easy, and all of a sudden there's that guy walking into the house next door. I realised he wasn't famous at all. He was just my neighbour. That's as close as I got to fame when I was in that cab!"

Did you ever doubt that Kiss would make it big?
Paul: "Never. Doubt is poison. Obstacles are what you see when you lose sight of your goals. It's like American football: you grab the ball, put your hand out in front of you, put your head down and start running forward. Anything that gets in the way goes down.

"Ultimately, you may lose a few battles but you win the war. Other people may have thought we weren't gonna make it, but failure was unacceptable to us."

Gene: "I'm delusional. I've always believed that – in the patois of our black brethren – I'm all that. Most people are afraid of ridicule. I want success so much that ridicule means absolutely nothing to me so long as there's just a glimmer of hope that I'll be wildly loved and worshipped and all the women will want to have my children. And that's what we all strive for, except there are few of us who are willing to scale the heights.

"Money, power? Delicious! I'm a whore for it. I fucking love it! I mean, how can anybody complain about touring? People will carry my luggage and if I want somebody to wipe my ass for me, they'll do it. All I have to do is get up onstage for two hours a night. Granted, it's hard physical work. And the rest of the time you can fuck, eat, sleep, do whatever you want."

What do you remember of your first meeting?
Gene: "I thought Paul was great. He thought I was a prick."

Kiss, 1981 (left to right) Gene Simmons, Eric Carr, Paul Stanley, Ace Frehley

Paul: "When I met Gene I didn't take well to him. He really was quite a prick. A mutual friend got us together. He was a guitar player and when he introduced us, he said, 'Why don't we put a band together?' I said, 'Well, you can have one with him or you can have one with me'. Famous last words! Ultimately we wound up playing together because we had a shared vision and philosophy. Although

"Most people are afraid of ridicule. I want success so much that ridicule means absolutely nothing to me so long as there's just a glimmer of hope that I'll be wildly loved and worshipped and all the women will want to have my children. And that's what we all strive for, except there are few of us

Kiss: the reformation (left to right) Gene Simmons, Peter Criss, Ace Frehley, Paul Stanley

we're totally different as people, the core, the work ethic, is very much the same.

"It's a great balance. That's the beauty of a great band: the volatility and the excitement of forces pulling in different directions."

In the mid 70s Kiss's work ethic was phenomenal. The band released six studio albums and two double-live sets in the first four years!

Paul: "We were so hungry for success. It's like a prizefighter on the way up, you take on all comers until you reach the top. Nowadays in boxing, a guy fights once every year, but there was a time when people fought every two months. With Kiss albums, if one didn't succeed or do as well as we wanted, we ran right back in the studio, finished another one and said, 'How about this?'

"*Kiss Alive!* was the album that broke us huge. It was exhilarating and it was frightening. To believe you're going to accomplish something and then see it happening is a bit overwhelming. Suddenly you look out into the audience and every night it is packed."

You were frightened by the scale of Kiss's success?
Paul: "Absolutely! Fame kills people. It's well documented. All of a sudden it's like a game show, when they open the curtain and there's your prize and – oh my God, it's bigger than I thought!

"The wild thing about success is that before you have it, you can only comprehend it in terms that you understand, so it's much narrower in scope, and then when you're immersed in it, it's a completely new world with no rules and you're king of the hill. It was exciting – a dangerous excitement – but I thought fame was a vehicle to enjoy your life, not to end it."

When Kiss became the biggest band in America, how did you keep your ego in check?

"I think I was an asshole sometimes, but not mean, probably just a bit full of myself, a bit catered to and pampered. The interesting thing about that is you don't even know it's happening. People around you insulate you. I never knew that our manager would tell everyone who came onboard how they should treat each one of us, what the do's and don'ts are. That's not how life works, so you end up with a slightly distorted view of who you are and what the world is. Again, it's all a learning experience, and I'm still here today."

Gene: "I thought our success was well deserved. I thought, 'Right, this is where we belong'. I know it comes off cocky when you read it back. Like, who does he think he is? Well, that's precisely the point. I really do think I'm all that and clearly the band is all that. I also thought we rose to the challenge. The band scaled the heights but we didn't stop. Once you become the pole-vaulting champion of the world, you don't just lean back because you're the champion. If you're a true champion, you try to better your own record, because you are a champion. We're in competition with nobody except ourselves."

What inspired Kiss to have the biggest and most outrageous stageshow in rock 'n' roll?
Paul: "Many kids at school would draw stage-sets with huge amplifiers. What we tried to do was make a reality of those fantasies we had about what a rock show could be. It's completely over the top and amazingly effective and entertaining. We've always done it for us. I'm not only in the band, I'm a big fan, and I want the band to do the kind of show that I want to see. When we're onstage, I know this is the shit. We are Kiss. Any band with money can have a Kiss show, but nobody else can be us. The 80s were full of Kiss shows with interchangeable bands, at times us included, but there's only one Kiss.

"I want every audience to feel that this is their night. And it is. The only night that counts is tonight. If someone's been waiting months to see you, what you did last night is of no consequence. If you're in bed with a woman, you want her to feel

that she's the best. You want to make everybody feel good. My God, look what those people made possible for us. So tonight is the only night that counts."

How did it feel when you first became rich?
Paul: "Money allows you to stop thinking about money. That's all. You're delusional if you think it's going to do more for you. It fucking well beats being poor, but other than that it's not a cure-all, a panacea. The best thing that money did for me is it allowed me to stop worrying about it.

"The first thing I bought when I got my first record deal at 15 was a clothes dryer for my mother. That's rock 'n' roll for you! At first I always bought things for my parents. I bought myself trinkets and stuff, but I bought my parents a car. They were good parents. They didn't have that much, we were fighting middle class. My parents never bought me an electric guitar. When they finally bought me a guitar, they got me a piece of crap that I wouldn't even pick up and play because I

"Many kids at school would draw stage-sets with huge amplifiers. **What we tried to do was make a reality of those fantasies we had about what a rock show could be. It's completely over the top and amazingly effective and entertaining.** We've always done it for us. I'm not only in the band, I'm a big fan, and I want the band to do the kind of show that I want to see."

was so angry. But my mother pawned a diamond ring to get me an amplifier, so as far as investments go, she did quite well, because after the car came a house.

"I'm very comfortable, obviously, but how many cars can you drive at one time? Unless you're gonna spread your legs apart and try to drive with one hand on each steering wheel, which I never tried. There's parts of my body I consider sacred.

"I have one car. In Los Angeles, go to the right supermarket and you'll see me shopping. If fame becomes a prison, what is the point of becoming famous? If people become successful and then complain about it, they surely don't deserve success. I whole-heartedly believe that the fans of those people would do them a great favour to stop supporting them. Let them go back to the kitchens they used to wash dishes in, where life is really good. Life at the top, I guess, is not for all.

"It's always amazing seeing people coming out of restaurants covering their faces because they don't want their picture taken, when a few years ago, they couldn't afford to eat in that restaurant. Let people take pictures. If you're in the public eye, if you don't want to be bothered, don't go out."

Gene: "The reason why the American message is accepted so readily by everybody in the four corners of the world is because it espouses those great universal truths which we all aspire to. Life is better worth living well than not, and aspiring to great-

ness doesn't mean that I'm better than you are, but that everybody should have a chance to get up there. The great American dream is that anybody can be President, anybody can be a millionaire. In America, you're damn right!"

When Kiss became successful in the 1970s, cocaine was rife in the music industry. What stopped you from getting into drink and drugs?

Paul: "A lot of it was common sense. Everybody knows if you jump off a building, it will kill you. I saw people die from drugs, I saw people lose all their creativity.

"I remember when I was 17 being at Electric Lady studio and some guy from a very big band was there with this huge vial of cocaine. I saw that guy's career and his vitality and spirit go down the toilet. Sex, drugs 'n' rock 'n' roll? All I wanted was the sex and the rock 'n' roll – you keep the drugs!

"I did small quantities of drugs when I was in my teens but I gotta say it was understandable at that point, because people didn't realise how dangerous drugs are. Now we all know. There's no excuse anymore. People who do drugs today are complete idiots. They're either trying to live a myth, or they're trying to be some caricature of what a rock 'n' roller is.

"I knew early on that I wanted success to be the key to having an awesome life, not an awesome death. There's nothing glamourous about being a dead legend. It may be a lot of fun for the people who buy your merchandise, but it doesn't leave a lot of room for you."

Gene: "It's very simple. We're Jews, aren't we? Well, if the world is trying to kill you, why help them? If your culture keeps espousing the notion that violence and drinking and all that is a sign of manhood, you might tend, although you have a choice, to go to bars and drink a lot and get into fights. But being Jewish or black or Pakistani is difficult enough without having the additional burden of having self-destructive habits. God bless the downtrodden people of the world. If you put in the time and overcome adversity, the racist school system and on and on, if you persevere and

> "I remember when I was 17 being at Electric Lady studio and some guy from a very big band was there with this huge vial of cocaine. I saw that guy's career and his vitality and spirit go down the toilet. Sex, drugs 'n' rock 'n' roll? **All I wanted was the sex and the rock 'n' roll – you keep the drugs!**"

KI77

"You drive us wild - we'll drive you crazy."

succeed, double the kudos.

"Why take drugs? Fuck that! What am I gonna do, help someone else kill me? I don't get it. And it costs money. Oh no! The idea is that money should come toward me, not go away."

How did it feel to watch Ace Frehley and Peter Criss succumb to booze and drugs and leave the band?
Paul: "It was sad. When somebody is drowning, you do your best to save them, but when they start to pull you under the water, you let go. You do what you can, but ultimately, it's up to all of us to save ourselves. Some people survive and some people don't. Some come around, some don't. I couldn't get enough sex, so the idea of drugs was just boring. There weren't enough hours in the day."

Sexually, how much have you experimented?
Paul: "Within the realm of female. I don't knock anybody for their preferences, but to me, there's

never been a second-best for a woman. It's not like,if I can't have a hamburger I guess I'll have a peanut butter sandwich. It doesn't quite work like that for me. I respect everybody's point of view, but, um, I like one flavour of ice cream.

"And there are lots of different ways to eat it. You can start at the bottom of the cone, you can start at the top, you can bite the middle...

"I looked at that whole gay scene as bizarre. I wanted to push the envelope – it was just a matter of which envelope. You know, I can remember being in bed with more that one woman who would say to me, 'My boyfriend says you're gay!', and I'd say, 'Well, guess why? He's afraid you'll show up here!'."

Gene: "There's absolutely no question that being in a rock band has its fringe benefits. If you were to take the negative point of view, 'Oh, they just want to be with you because you're in a band'. Okay. Who cares? When you win the Lottery and someone says, 'There's no talent involved in that,' you say, 'Fuck you – whoopee! I got lots of money.' So, Whoopee! I got lots of ass! Who cares?

"I fuck anything that moves. And I mean that in the nicest way. That's really the biggest kick, that a guy who looks like me can get laid. That's astonishing to me. Think about it. If there are uglier guys around I don't know where they are, and yet I am the king of puss, boy!"

Gene, are you still photographing all the women you sleep with?
Gene: "Well, I have 4,600 photos. They run the gamut. There's been fruit, flagpoles. There's one wonderful picture of a girl hanging from the second floor of a hotel from a flagpole, right near the American flag, she's completely nude. People were pointing from the street. It was an urge, call it what you will. She couldn't get down. The firetruck was called. It's all fun and games. Let's face it: if I was a dentist it wouldn't quite be the same."

Have you ever had an AIDS test?
Paul: "Oh yeah. The first one by far and away was the scariest. When this revelation came that what you had done for the last ten years could now kill you, I just about lost my lunch. Wait a minute: you didn't tell me those were the rules. I've been playing this game for ten years, and nobody told me that striking out means dying. So the first AIDS test was a very long wait. In hindsight, there are things that I've done which, knowing what I know today, were rather daring."

Have you ever been hurt onstage?
Paul: "I broke a rib. Normal stuff, it happens to everybody. I broke a rib running into a guard rail onstage. I could feel it snap. I just kept going due to the adrenaline. The next morning I woke up and

"We have no illusions about any of it meaning anything. It means nothing. When there's a big fireworks display on Guy Fawkes Night or the Fourth of July, everything's blowing up in the sky and everyone's going, 'Wow', and a critic comes over and says, 'Yes, but what does it mean?'. This guy's on crack! He can't even enjoy the simple things in life without contemplating the eternal navel. Girls do it. You've just enjoyed wonderful sex, and she gets up and says, 'What does this mean?'. **It means I had a day of pleasure. I was glad to be alive one more day. That's all."**

"The wild thing about success is that before you have it, you can only comprehend it in terms that you understand, so it's much narrower in scope, and then when you're immersed in it, **it's a completely new world with no rules and you're king of the hill. It was exciting – a dangerous excitement –** but I thought fame was a vehicle to enjoy your life, not to end it."

I tried to get out of bed and I couldn't move. I've had surgery on both my knees, [and] a shoulder. I'm on my way to becoming bionic!"

Is it hard work playing a Kiss show?
Gene: "Being onstage is a Jekyll and Hyde thing.

Purging. It's very freeing. It's like when you're fucking for a long time, the third or fourth time, and you're not orgasming yet, and you just go, for fuck's sake, just shoot the splurge! When it finally comes you go, 'Ahh, there you go'."

Back in the 70s, you were branded Satanists. Somebody even claimed that the band's name stood for Knights In Satan's Service! Did you just laugh it off?
Paul: "I was gonna say it was just a pinheaded evangelist, but they're much smarter than that. When people would accuse us of stuff, it had very little to do with us. It had more to do with them getting some airtime. It was very self-serving. I was amazed, because having thought of the name Kiss, I certainly didn't consider myself bright enough to come up one that had initials that stood for something!"

Are you happy that Kiss Meets The Phantom Of The Park, the band's 1970s movie, is now revered as a kitsch classic?
Paul: "Kiss Meets The Phantom... is a very funny film, it just wasn't meant to be. We were told that we were gonna make a film that was going to be a cross between A Hard Day's Night and Star Wars. Hey, sounds like a winner to me!

"But none of us had a clue what acting was, conceptually or otherwise, and most of the band never read the script. So we'd show up each day and someone would throw our lines to us off-camera, then they would roll film and we'd say the lines, and if we got the line right, they kept it! This wasn't Hamlet, it was four idiots in front of a camera!

"About midway through it we all had this notion that this was really going terribly wrong. I remember saying to our manager, I'm really scared, this seems to really suck, and he said, 'Oh, no no no – this is gonna be great!'. And sure enough, they had a screening for it before it aired on television in America, and by the time it was over I was almost under my chair! I didn't want anybody to see me. Then you have all these Hollywood types coming over. 'Oh, babe – loved you!'. And you're thinking, it's more insulting to me that you just don't say, 'What a piece of shit,' cos then at least we could have a laugh together.

"Ultimately, it's such a bizarrre film that it has an enormous cult following. And kitsch was never a word we would have used in describing it before we made it. We're right up there with Ed Wood!"

Kiss have always had a fanatical following, but have never received critical acclaim. Does that anger you?
Gene: "Credibility and cowardice both start with the letter 'c' and both revolve on the same principle, which is: you're afraid of what you want to do because what would people think? What a fucking load of crap!

"You're a band and you're thinking, let's take a picture in front of that whorehouse, but then you think, you probably shouldn't, because what would people think? We'd lose our credibility.

"I don't care! We have no credibility, we want no credibility. Fuck your credibility! We're very American in a very simple sense: of the people, for the people, by the people.

"A critic's opinion doesn't matter to me anywhere near as much as somebody who pays for a ticket. A food critic will never appreciate food as much as the guy who has to earn the money to buy that hotdog on the street corner. To him, it's the most delicious meal he'll ever have, and the food critic will say, 'Well, it's a bit heavy on the grease and not quite as good as down the street'. It's a warped point of view. You can never appreciate a drink of water, a simple glass of water, unless you're thirsty. Then it means something. So it's the people, always, who determine our style."

Is is true that Kiss make more money from merchandise than from records?
Gene: "Sometimes, yeah. Both make enormous amounts, and I'm thrilled, happy and grateful to be filthy rich and getting enormously richer by the day!"

Is the Kiss car, at over $70,000, the biggest piece of Kiss merchandise at present?
Gene: "For now. But next comes Kisstianity, of course. It sounds better than the other religions, I think. There's only one rule: don't hurt anybody. That's the rule. Isn't that nice? Don't hurt anybody, physically, psychologically, whatever."

Pearl Jam's Eddie Vedder: unimpressed by Gene Simmons' lunchbox

What other merchandise is coming?
Gene: "Everything that we can do that REM and Pearl Jam and a million other bands can't. Those bands make great music. Radiohead? Fabulous. But they'll never make a lunchbox or a bubblegum card, and we revel in that. We're the only ones who can do it. We're going to have a Kiss cartoon show and everything, and I love the fact that those other bands are fucking scared to death of doing bubblegum cards and comic books. I think, what cowards.

"I'm a big fan of Eddie Vedder and Pearl Jam. I went to see them in Los Angeles, and two of those guys are card-carrying members. Fair enough, I'm not tugging at your shirtsleeves here saying, 'Look, look, they like us!'.

"But I have a fascination with anybody who wants to prevent the life experience from being

Wolfgang Amadeus Mozart: "a commercial artist" - just like Kiss!

full. I don't understand it. I also don't understand suicide. Why would anybody want to end their life when every day above ground is a gloriously wonderful day? I can't understand anybody who doesn't get that. You may have to dig ditches on a highway, but when you get back home you have a great meal, you have a woman in bed . . . all those things that make life worth living.

"So I'm speaking to one of the guys in Pearl Jam, Stone Gossard, and I said, 'You know, this is a lot of fun. Your fans obviously enjoy this, but you hardly tour. Why don't you tour more, make more fans happy.' He says, 'No, I wanna go skiing.' I thought that was bizarre concept. Whatever happened to the work ethic?

"This is your job. It's less about what you want to do and even less about what you like. My point of view is: you shouldn't necessarily have to like what you do, even as an artist. Rembrandt was asked to paint portraits of political figures in his time; Mozart was told what to do, how long his piano concertos should be, and he was paid for it. They were commercial artists. Michaelangelo was told how to paint that ceiling, put God over there . . . they were told what to do. That's their job. Like comicbook artists or jingle writers, except those people have no credibility.

"It's only the spoiled artists who says, 'I don't feel like that, because I don't feel inspiration.' Fuck your inspiration! Put in the time. This is your job. You work for me: please me, I'm paying you money. And that's our philosophy. The fans are the bosses. I work for you. What do you want? The artists who don't care what the fans want, who only do what they want to do, are delusional."

Is is true that on Kiss's reunion tour, Ace and Peter were paid a wage while Gene and Paul shared most of the profits?
Gene: "It's fair that anybody can have their point of view about anything, but Ace and Peter have been every bit as important as anybody else. No matter what you think your contribution is to an entity, certain things are not possible unless other things are set up. Ace designed the original logo,

Paul thought of the name, Peter wrote "Beth", and all those little pieces make up the big puzzle. And no matter how many pieces of the puzzle you think you put on the board, if there's one little piece missing, it's not complete.

"It is true that all four of us are sitting in the same car, and we're all going the same way, but not everybody can drive the car. Two guys can sit in the front, two guys can sit in the back, and when you take a step back, it's a car moving forward. It is a group entity. Take your pick on what that means."

Can you explain why Kiss has remained so successful for so long?
Paul: "Ultimately, there's a niche for us, and no-one has come along who can do it better, and they won't, because by the time that happens we'll be gone.

"I think I was an asshole sometimes, but not mean, probably just a bit full of myself, a bit catered to and pampered. The interesting thing about that is you don't even know it's happening. People around you insulate you. I never knew that our manager would tell everyone who came onboard how they should treat each one of us, what the do's and don'ts are. That's not how life works, so you end up with a slightly distorted view of who you are and what the world is. Again, it's all a learning experience, and I'm still here today."

There's nothing worse than seeing someone onstage who's a shadow of what they once were. I never want to go onstage and have people say, 'Remember when he was good?', or 'Remember when he didn't have that belly?'. The day I take my shirt off and someone says, 'Put it back on,' I'm on the plane back home!"

Gene: "We have no illusions about any of it meaning anything. It means nothing. When there's a big fireworks display on Guy Fawkes Night or the Fourth of July, everything's blowing up in the sky and everyone's going, 'Wow', and a critic comes over and says, 'Yes, but what does it mean?'. This guy's on crack! He can't even enjoy the simple things in life without contemplating the eternal navel.

"Whether you understand Kiss or not, you either get it in your heart or you don't. We're clowns. Okay. Are you gonna buy a ticket or not? Ultimately that speaks louder than words, because either you think it's worth your hard-earned money, or you don't.

"Trust me, I love the sound of my own voice and reading about myself in magazines, I fucking love it. I'm so interested. I'm delusional, and that has its advantages, because you actually love reading all the things you say.

"We really do believe in the great work ethic and we believe that we have a responsibility to live up to this sort of silly notion that if you wanted the best, you got the best. Living up to that is our responsibility: 'The Hottest Band In The World.' How much crack would we have to be on to put that in front of us if we weren't gonna go out there and deliver? If you know that you're gonna go out there and coast, don't introduce yourself as 'The Hottest Band In The World'!

"We have no illusions about any of it meaning anything: it means nothing. Girls do it. You've just enjoyed wonderful sex, and she gets up and says, 'What does this mean?'. It means I had a day of pleasure. I was glad to be alive one more day. That's all."

Paul Stanley: nobody does it better

Nobody forgets the first time they saw a
picture of Kiss or heard a Kiss record.
And for the people who speak here, their first
Kiss was the beginning of a lifelong love affair.

"KISS CHANGED MY LIFE!"

For many Kiss fans in the UK, their introduction to "The Hottest Band In The World" came via the pages of the now defunct rock magazine *Sounds* and the writing of Geoff Barton, a manic Kiss fan himself who went on to launch the world's foremost metal magazine *Kerrang!*. Several of the fans interviewed here – Howard Johnson, Dave Reynolds, Joe Mackett and the author – played alongside Geoff Barton in *Kerrang!*'s semi-legendary football team, Inter Kerrang! All owe a debt to Geoff for his unceasing support of the band. Kiss fans are a funny bunch. And these are their stories . . .

Gary Banton

Gary Banton plays Gene Simmons in the top Kiss tribute band Dressed To Kill. He lives in Wimbledon, London.

"It was February 1982, I was 10 years old and my folks and I were visiting family in Melbourne, Australia. Adam had taken Marco and just dumped the rest of his Ants! I was in severe shock! No more Gary Tibbs, Merrick and Terry Lee Miall? It didn't bear thinking about! Luckily my Aussie cousin Pete had a major surprise waiting for me; one that would change my life.

'Forget Adam & The Ants,' he said, 'check these guys out!' I looked up in awe at the posters that covered his walls. There was a bloke with a big pout and a star on his eye, a spaceman with a silver explosion on his face, a cool looking guy with a Zorro-style eye mask (a fox, apparently!) and a mean looking vampire-type dude with a costume made of what looked like solid rock! There were also a couple of pictures of another guy with a cat face. 'Wow!' I exclaimed. 'Who are they?!' 'Don't you know Kiss?!' he replied in disbelief as he cued up a record on his turntable, 'They rock!' As the opening audience noise, guitar riffs and the pyrotechnic bangs of 'Detroit Rock City' rang out from side one of *Alive II*, I thought to myself, 'They certainly do!'

"There began an unstoppable chain of events. As soon as we got back home to England I rushed down to Our Price on Wimbledon Broadway and immediately bought *Unmasked*, soon to be followed by *Kiss*, *Destroyer* and *Killers*. By now I lived and breathed Kiss music. On my next birthday I found myself dragging my Dad up to the old Virgin Megastore on Oxford Street. With much

"My Saturday afternoons generally consisted of loitering in record shops. One day I was browsing through the 'K' section when I came came across the Holy Grail of live albums, *Alive II*. When I opened up the gatefold sleeve my love affair with Kiss truly began. Flames, make-up, a stage design that blew my adolescent mind! Kiss were my new favourite rock lords"

excitement I extracted a copy of *Alive II* from the rack and presented it to my Dad for purchasing! Happy Birthday to me! We then stopped for lunch in McDonalds and I remember pulling the shrink-wrap off and opening the gatefold to expose Kiss in all their live glory. A picture and a moment that will always be special to me. I wanted to see that, and somewhere in the back of my mind I realised that I wanted to do that! I also received an acoustic guitar and weekly lessons for my birthday, and of course there was only one band I really wanted to learn how to play like!

Now there was no stopping me and I saved up my pocket money to buy all the albums and as many posters, badges, postcards, patches and magazines featuring Kiss as I could afford! There

was even a great heavy-sounding new album, *Creatures Of The Night*.

"At this point, I thought Gene was the coolest, with Ace a close second. Unfortunately, Ace was out and some new guy called Vinnie Vincent was in. At first I was distraught, but when I realised that most of the superb guitar playing on *Creatures . . .* was Vinnie I soon started smiling again. My relief from upheaval was shortlived though when it was announced that Kiss were unmasking for the next album and tour. No way! They can't do this! Nevertheless, on the day of release, I rushed down to good old Our Price to buy the new album *Lick It Up* and to finally see what they really looked like!

"Well, Gene and Paul looked very cool. Eric had so much hair and looked great (he had by now become my second fave since Ace left), but who/what the hell was that other guy?! Yikes! Vinnie Vincent really shouldn't have unmasked. He looked like a fish!

"The album sounded great and I was a very happy bunny, but I still hadn't seen them live. But that was about to change as they announced a tour including Wembley Arena in October! I had to go, but there was no way my folks were gonna let me go alone, so I dragged both my parents to the show and finally converted them after 18 months of blasting Kiss out of my room! Sadly, with the

The Kiss tribute act Dressed To Kill starring Gary Banton as Gene

Gene Simmons: not Gary Banton!

passage of time I don't remember too much of the show now (I was wide-eyed and open mouthed for most of it), but I do remember the loud bangs and the laxative effect that Gene's bass frequencies had on my bowels! Cool!

"Throughout the 80s I continued in my almost blind adoration of the band, and around 1988 I became involved with the new UK Kiss fan club KISS Crazy. At first I just submitted articles but I subsequently became the Assistant Editor and revelled in all the perks that this offered. The first of these was when I received a handwritten Happy Birthday message from Gene Simmons on my 18th birthday! Of course I framed that and it went straight up on my wall!

"Around this time I also met Ashley Brookes, who was a huge Kiss fan and a Paul Stanley look-alike. We chatted about trying to set up a copy/tribute band and decided to give it a go. Advertising in KISS Crazy for an Ace Frehley and a Peter Criss or Eric Carr, we subsequently found our other two members in Dave 'Pat' Patterson and

Richard Sawyer. Having chosen a song list and set a date for rehearsal we finally got together and blasted through a number of Kiss classics. Though we were very rough around the edges we decided that with some work musically and some investment in costumes we should give it a go! The name, Dressed To Kill (after their third LP), was decided upon and once the Love Gun costumes (the best ones) were made and a setlist decided, we launched ourselves on an unsuspecting public, debuting with a three-page gig review spread in *Kerrang!* magazine. More than 12 years later and we are still going strong, touring throughout the UK and Europe. We have also completed a huge two-week tour of Japan, including a show at the massive Ariake Coliseum in Tokyo! Our show now includes the smoking guitar, firebreathing, pyrotechnics and even identical instruments to Kiss. Thousands of pounds have been spent to enhance the production and this, along with our extensive experience and commitment to accuracy, have made us Europe's #1 Kiss tribute band.

"We've had some funny times with Dressed To Kill. We travelled to Austria to play a biker festival and found ourselves faced with hundreds of European bikers and Hells Angels who hardly clapped between songs. Thinking that if we're gonna die, we might as well make it quick, we played the Kiss disco anthem 'I Was Made For Lovin' You' and prepared to run for our lives! To our utter disbelief the crowd went crazy, dancing

> **"The cool thing was that each Kiss member was so different from the others that you could have your favourite.** This was also the appeal the Spice Girls would have in the 1990s, although, er, not quite in the same way as the hottest band in the world"

"'Has Genie told you what I used to call him?' she giggled. We shook our heads and Gene hid behind a curtain in the hotel hallway pleading with her not to embarrass him in front of his fans! **'I used to call him Puppy!'** "

and singing, climbing on tables and chanting along! Returning to our traditional little village hotel afterward (still fully made-up), we found the whole village having a get-together on the lawn. When they saw us, they welcomed us with open arms and we found ourselves dancing with a traditional oom-pah band. It seemed the locals believed we really were Kiss! A young woman approached me and pointed to her son who was sitting wide-eyed and smiling in a wheelchair. She told us that he was mentally and physically disabled but a huge Kiss fan and that, though she knew we were not them, he believed we were. She asked us to pretend we were them as it would make him the happiest boy in the world. Our initial reluctance was overcome as soon as we saw him reach his hands out to us with a big grin on his face. Choked with emotion we knelt down beside him, held his hands, gave him plectrums and had our photo taken with him. You have never seen four more humbled individuals than us as we returned to our hotel rooms afterward.

"On a separate visit to Vienna, in conjunction with Mercury Records, to promote Kiss's *Psycho Circus* album, we happily chatted and signed photos, etc. for fans after our show. One guy, however, opened a bag and produced his entire Kiss vinyl collection for us to sign! We protested, 'But we aren't Kiss! We don't want to deface or devalue your records!', but were simply met with the repetitive response, 'You sign! You sign! Please!' He wouldn't leave us alone so we ended up signing them just to move him along. Oh dear!

"In 1990 I was given the opportunity to follow Kiss on tour in the USA at the end of their Hot In The Shade tour. Carol (who ran the fan club) and I flew to North Carolina to see the last three shows of the tour. Little did I know at the time, but these were to be the last three shows that Eric Carr ever performed with Kiss.

"We started in Asheville NC, where we stayed in the same hotel as them! Eric and Bruce said 'Hi!' at breakfast and we were given VIP laminates for the shows by the tour manager. I finally met Gene backstage and he was very gracious and then I met

Eric again in the hotel bar (I shouldn't have been there as I was still underage) where he bought me a beer. He was a lovely guy, so unassuming, and I miss him to this day.

"The next town was Herschey PA, where I finally met Paul backstage and pissed him off by asking him to sign some stuff with an old marker pen which proceeded to leak all over his hands! Sorry Paul! The last show was the final date of the tour at Madison Square Garden in New York. What a venue and what a show! Backstage I met Gene's mother and various well known rockers including Joe Lynn Turner. This trip was to be one I would never forget.

"I continued my fandom through the early 1990s and was completely knocked for six by the death of the great Eric Carr. He was such a genuine guy with a heart of gold, and he never received the credit he was due. Even in death, he had the misfortune to pass away on the same day as Freddie Mercury of Queen, thereby confining himself to a small note in the corner of the page.

"A couple of years later Gene and Paul were in London on a stop on their promotional tour and staying in an exclusive hotel behind Park Lane. Some European Kiss fans/friends of mine had found out where they were staying, and booked the room next door to Gene so I went up to visit them. To the best of my recollection the following is what happened.

"As we were sitting and chatting there was a knock on the door and one of the fans went to open it. Gene strode into the room and said 'Hi' to everyone. 'You guys wanna meet Cher? She's staying in a room upstairs.' 'Yes, please!' We followed Gene to her room and she opened the door looking so natural! Her long, black hair lay straight and centre-parted, and she was barefoot with denim dungarees covering a white cut-off T-shirt. She said 'Hi' and shook all of our hands. What followed were some of the most amazing conversations I've ever heard. It was like we weren't even there! Gene and Cher chatted openly and obviously still had a lot of affection for each other. 'Has Genie told you what I used to call him?' she giggled. We shook

"He emerged from the dressing room in full regalia roaring and shouting 'Oh yeah', and he towered over me sticking his tongue out. I thought he was being ridiculous so **I slapped his face and said, 'Genie, don't be so silly!'** He stood there stunned and it took him a couple of minutes to get back in character for the show!" cher

our heads and Gene hid behind a curtain in the hotel hallway pleading with her not to embarrass him in front of his fans! 'I used to call him Puppy!' We fell about laughing and pointing at Gene, who cringed and let out a long, pained 'Noooo!'. Hilarious!

"She then went on to tell us about the first Kiss show she ever went to. 'I was in the backstage area and Gene told me not to be frightened of him when he finally came out of the dressing room before the show. He said he would be in character, very loud and overpowering and I might be afraid of him. Sure enough he emerged from the dressing room in full regalia roaring and shouting "Oh yeah!", and he towered over me sticking his tongue out. I thought he was being ridiculous so I slapped his face and said, "Genie, don't be so silly!" He stood there stunned and it took him a couple of minutes to get back in character for the show!'

"Throughout this hilarious story Gene was cringing and hiding behind the curtain, going very red-faced with embarrassment. Cher was charming and it was touching to see Gene in a more natural, laid back moment. I feel lucky to have been there.

"One of the perks of being in a Kiss tribute band is that we are acknowledged by Kiss and even get the chance to play with a member/ex-

member of the band on occasion. However, this is not always a pleasure. One such occasion was at the 1994 Kiss Convention at the London Astoria 2. Peter Criss was the special guest for the day and it had been pre-agreed that he would join us on stage for three songs. Our own 'Peter Criss', Rich, was in complete awe and couldn't believe that his hero would be playing his drum kit! When the time came, Peter came onstage and got comfortable behind the kit. We launched into 'Deuce', with Peter missing his cue at the start. He then played the song too slowly, and held the groove back before forgetting his final drum roll to end the song! Oh dear! Next up was 'Strutter', which he played a little better but ended wrongly, and finally it was 'Firehouse', which he played OK. It was spooky seeing the real Peter Criss sitting at the drums and playing with him but I must admit, as a bassist, it was a relief to get my drummer back and get the groove happening again! Indeed, Dave Reynolds noted in *Kerrang!* magazine that our drummer made a welcome return to the stage!

"Like everyone else I was thrilled when Kiss reformed the original line-up and put the make-up back on. Finally, I would get a chance to see the full 1970's style pyrotechnic stage show, although I wondered whether the reunion would have happened had Eric Carr still been alive, or whether it would have just been a reunion with Ace. After all, Eric Carr was a fan favourite and one helluva nice guy and if he had been sidelined I don't know how the fans would have reacted. The first UK show at Donington was a highlight; they blew the place apart. Courtesy of our contact at Mercury Records UK, me and my girlfriend of the time went backstage at Wembley Arena on the tour that followed. Naturally, Gene tried to steal my girlfriend. Later, Kiss manager Doc McGhee invited us all back to the hotel bar. The band had disappeared up to their rooms, but Doc ordered some champagne for us and was a very gracious host. I asked why they weren't playing 'Beth' and he told me that they didn't believe it would work outside of the

US. I assured him that it would work, that it was as much a part of the show as the blood spitting, the fire breathing and the smoking guitar. Lo and behold, as the band continued their European tour they had, within days, introduced the song into the set! Who says that they don't listen to their fans?

"I'm still a big fan, my memorabilia collection is still spreading throughout my home and Dressed To Kill have gone from strength to strength. We are in our twelfth year and you can catch us at a venue near you!

"We have a basic webpage at:http://www. kiss-inuk. com/tribdtk.htm."

Dante Bonutto

A marketing and promotional consultant at Universal Music International, Dante has interviewed Kiss on numerous occasions for Kerrang! *and* RAW *magazines.*

"When I was at school and getting into rock music, I sampled every music magazine and I loved *Sounds*. Geoff Barton wrote all the metal stuff. He got me into Rush, lots of obscure Canadian bands, and certainly Kiss. *Alive II* was the first Kiss album I got and it's one of the greatest-packaged records of all time. It was bought for me as a Christmas present and I remember finding it in a cupboard and opening it before Christmas Day. It's quite sad, really, because I wasn't that young then. It was definitely a life-changing experience. The Casablanca label alone was quite exciting, and of course, when you learned more about it, it was a very exciting label, probably for all the wrong reasons. Record companies aren't like that anymore.

"The whole concept of Kiss was great. At first my favourite member of the group was Paul Stanley, although now, having met them all, I would say Ace Frehley. When I worked for *Kerrang!* we recreated the cover of *Lick It Up* and I chose the Paul Stanley role, almost instinctively.

"Once I got to like Kiss I wanted to meet them, like every fan. I'd done a degree in media studies and was offered a job at Spotlight Publications, who published *Sounds*. I thought I'd have Geoff Barton's job in a matter of days, but unfortunately I was sent for training at *Accountants Weekly*! I was dreadful. Then I was moved to a medical magazine called *Pulse* and was writing about operations. I had to get away, so I contacted a musicians' magazine and asked them if they'd like a piece on Kiss. They assumed I'd written loads of stuff before so they said yes. I paid my own airfare to New York and set up the interview with their PR person.

This was 1981 when *The Elder* was about to come out. They had short hair, which I didn't realise at the time. I was sitting in the reception at Aucoin Management. It was an enormous office,

Then they took me into this huge room and showed me a model of the stage set for *The Elder*. It was all pyramids and turrets and little figures of themselves. It was never built, of course, because the album didn't do as well as they hoped. They said they were going to record the whole album live, although they did none of it live as it turned out. It was very impressive, this huge office with gold discs everywhere. For me it was like a grotto. I had always associated Kiss so much with New York, I was pleased to have met them there. It was a thrill.

"When I went on to *Kerrang!*, I always did the Kiss interviews. I spoke to Peter Criss on the phone and he was really rude to me. He said, 'Why don't

> "A very good friend of mine in the States, Jason Loeb, got married to a girl whose maiden name is Andrea Stanley. She was expecting their first baby and **there's a tradition in the family that if the child is a boy, the middle name is Stanley.** Jason convinced her to call the baby Paul. He phoned me one night and said, 'She's agreed', and I knew exactly what he was talking about. A day later they were sitting at home watching TV and **she looked at him and said, 'No!'.** He said, 'What are you talking about?', and **she says, 'Paul Stanley** – no!'."

so big that Chrysalis Records bought it later. This bloke walked by with short hair. It was Paul Stanley but I didn't recognise him at first. I was ushered inside and met Paul and he looked exactly as I'd imagined he would without make-up. He played me some of the new tracks. The first track he played was 'I'. Gene Simmons walked in the room and started singing the song. I turned around and thought, 'Who's this?'. This bloke with dark skin. He looked nothing like I thought he would. I was quite shocked.

"I interviewed the pair of them. We talked a little about guitars to keep this magazine happy.

you just fuck right off! I'm sick and tired of being bothered by people like you.' I said, 'Actually, I work for a music magazine and I'm really interested in your drumming skills.' He said, 'Oh, sorry. I'm just sick of paparazzi.'

"I spent months tracking down Ace for a *Kerrang!* cover story, and he was very entertaining, I must say. I have a lot of respect for Paul Stanley because a lot of the times when I interviewed Kiss, it was often him in the studio alone while Simmons was off in LA acting. It's Paul who kept the band going in those dark days, but Frehley was certainly the human face of Kiss. The others didn't indulge

Bruce Kulick (left) and Gene Simmons

in all the kinds of things you might have thought they would have done, whereas Ace was clearly the rock 'n' roll character. I remember asking Gene Simmons why he didn't drink. He said he didn't want to smell like Ace Frehley. Gene also said that Peter Criss would frighten himself if he saw his own reflection in a shop window, his mind has wandered so far.

"Gene and Paul are like a double act; they're very funny and they obviously have some regard for each other deep down. The only time I found it tough interviewing Kiss was when they came to the UK to do promotion for *Creatures Of The Night* and they brought Ace with them. I asked Ace if he played on the album, but he skirted around that very simple question, to put it mildly!

"The whole *Creatures . . .* album means a lot to me. I'd gone to Hawaii for Ozzy Osbourne's wedding and on the way back I had to go through LA where Kiss were recording at the Record Plant, so I called the band's management and we set up an interview for the cover of *Kerrang!*. When I got to the studio Paul Stanley was in shorts. Simmons wasn't, of course. He was in leather. And Eric Carr floated in. They were all saying, 'Oh, you just missed Ace'. Again, they had a cardboard mock-up of the stage set. I was always destined to see these things. And it was a little cardboard tank. Simmons told me I must not tell anybody about the tank; it was top secret.

"When they unmasked, they called me up and told me they were taking the make-up off. I used to get the news about things like Mark Norton leaving. I was kept in the loop. I used to wait for these calls. I flew to New York in a panic and walked in thinking it was a joke, but on a long table they'd spread out all their press shots, so I knew they were serious about taking the make-up off.

"Ross Halfin and I went to Texas to see Kiss – Gene Simmons always wore cowboy boots. Ross and I had never owned a pair. Simmons told us he's introduce us to the world of the cowboy boot. The band's hotel had a shop that sold them, so we walked in there and the woman in the shop completely lost it. Simmons obviously has amazing charisma. He gave her passes for the show and we got two free pairs of cowboy boots. When I interviewed Gene the next day I went to his hotel room and he had the girl from the shop on his bed. It was all very rock 'n' roll. It was great."

Tony Cooke

Managing Director of music PR company LD Publicity, Tony Cooke is the former drummer in glam metal band Rag Dolls.

"Kiss are my favourite band ever, and will always be so. When I lived in Manchester, I was a drummer in a metal band, not a very good one, called the Rag Dolls. We never achieved very much. I was into lots of bands that nobody had ever heard of, all the 'New Wave Of British Heavy Metal' bands, Tygers Of Pan Tang, Mythra, Angel Witch, etc.

"I was a metalhead. I had a mullet and I wore spandex, even though I've always been a bit too fat to wear it. I'd go to rock clubs but sometimes I'd dip out, put my smart clothes on and go to the disco because that's where the girls were. It was a different kind of scene, but I was quite happy there getting pissed and looking at nice foxy ladies in short skirts and listening to Kiss's disco song 'I Was Made For Lovin' You'.

"I got into the whole image of Kiss, and Yanks Records in Manchester had all the Kiss albums on import. You could walk out with ten albums for a fiver. That's how I got *Alive II*. And I couldn't believe it when I opened up the gatefold sleeve. Kiss was a phenomenon. I had to discover what it was all about. I was a drummer and Peter Criss had a drum-riser that was fifty feet high. I was mesmerised.

"Kiss had so much mystique, but when they unmasked, I didn't want them to do it. When I saw Kiss in 1984 I'd gone to see the support act, which was Bon Jovi, but Kiss really blew me away.

"Mark and Lard, the Radio 1 DJs, used to play 'Crazy Crazy Nights' every week and each time they played it they'd mention me because I'd taken them to see Kiss in Manchester in 1995. They only lasted two songs. I was supposed to be treating them to a Chinese meal, but I stayed at the gig and gave them the money. I never saw them again but every time they play a Kiss song they talked about that night.

"I bought Paul's guitar recently for a bargain price. There's a little bit of a scratch on it, so it's probably been played for three minutes. It's signed by Ace, Peter, Gene and Paul. I paid hundreds of pounds. I was offered a lot of money for it the day after I bought it, from someone at the Hard Rock Cafe, but I would never sell it. My kids will probably take it to a car boot sale when I'm 60 and in a wheelchair."

Chris Dale

A member of UK rock band Sack Trick and of Iron Maiden singer Bruce Dickinson's touring band, Chris Dale is currently recording a Kiss tribute album.

"I was 13 when I first got into Kiss. A mate of mine over the road had *Alive II*. I had to get all the albums after that. There was a second-hand record shop where I lived in Lampeter, in West Wales, and luckily Kiss are quite popular in the second-hand shops.

"The first gig I ever went to was Kiss on the *Lick It Up* tour. I was dead excited when I got the tickets, but I'd bought them before they announced they were taking the make-up off. I was horrified when I saw the album cover in the shop, but it was still an amazing gig. And I met them in the afternoon. They arrived at Wembley Arena in a couple of limos and they stopped to sign autographs. They didn't have to do that, did they? I just stared at them. I was in awe. I didn't get anything signed.

"I met Ace at a signing session for Frehley's Comet. I took a copy of 'What Makes The World Go 'Round', the single from *Unmasked*. It had a picture of Ace on the cover with a smoking guitar. I got that signed, but he said, 'So what is it?'. I'm like, 'Well, it's your single!'. He asked me, 'How does it go?' So I sang a bit of the chorus and he said, 'No, don't know it – next!' Did he really not know that song? And was it really necessary to humiliate a nervous fan? Yes, it probably was in his bored afternoon!

"To say that Kiss have played a major part in my life is an understatement. I thought I would grow out of it, but there's no sign of that happening yet. I was in Amsterdam recently and found some Kiss collectors' cards in a fantasy book shop. **I got so excited, my wife nearly died of embarrassment!**"

"Obviously after the gig I was waiting around, stalking, outside Hammersmith Odeon, and Ace came out and threw a bunch of plectrums on the floor. It was a clever idea. Everybody scrambled around on the floor trying to get a plectrum and he gets in the limo. I read later that Ace often did the same thing with dollar bills and laughed at people picking them up. Then you realise he actually does have quite a nasty sense of humour.

"Kiss are my all-time favourite band. No one else comes close. I went through a phase at school of listening to other bands – Maiden, AC/DC, Accept, Mötley Crüe. Then one day I listened to *Alive II* again and gave up on all the other bands on the spot. None of them have got 'Shout It Out Loud'.

"Kiss have the best image in the world, amazing songs, and there's always hilarious things going on. I'm not sure how much Kiss get the joke themselves. I think maybe in Britain there's a different following. We're laughing at it, but also with it, because we're the fans.

"I've got a Kiss marble. I never saw the purpose of it but I've still got it. It sits on a shelf. Nobody else is allowed to touch it. My Vinnie Vincent plectrum is the ultimate bit of Kiss memorabilia. It's quite rare. My friend caught it at Bingley Hall in Stafford. I roadied for his band for free to get the plectrum off him. Normally I'd charge proper money, so ultimately it cost me about £70.

"My band Sack Trick are doing a Kiss tribute album. Obviously people have done this before, but you only get one chance in life to do a Kiss tribute album. On the other hand, there's a lot of material. We want to make it the best Kiss tribute ever. We're doing the whole of *The Elder*. It's very silly. It's taken us longer to re-record *The Elder* than it took them to do it originally. Leigh from Terrorvision is doing 'Mr Blackwell'. He's so evil!

"The album is called *Sheep In Kiss Make-Up*. You know how sheep have blotchy black and white faces? If their blotches were moved just a little, it's quite close. *The Elder* is performed as one song, a 20-minute medley. Just the salient points. We've done the fanfare on recorders. We've got a reggae 'Love Gun'. We've got a Spanish waiter singing 'I'm A Legend Tonight'. 'Almost Human' with a robot voice – because he's not quite human, is he? We've got a Cornish fisherman doing 'War Machine'. He also plays bass in Emma Bunton's band. And we've done 'Shout It Out Loud', which features loads of different singers. Bruce Dickinson's on it.

"My favourite Kiss member varies. You take it for granted that Gene and Paul are there, so I go for Ace quite a lot. I've also got soft spots for Eric Carr and Vinnie Vincent, because they were in the band when I was getting into them. Their make-up was brilliant. And the hawk thing. First they tried putting Eric Carr in hawk make-up and he hated it and did his own make-up.

"Then there was an interview with Vinnie and he said he thought about being a hawk. Obviously Gene had told him. And years later there was a brilliant interview with Eric Singer where he said he wondered what make-up he would have had. He said he asked Gene one day and Gene said perhaps he could have been a hawk!

"The one problem I have with Kiss is this: I'm very much in love with my girlfriend Dawn but she's the first person in my life who's put a limit on the number of Kiss posters I'm allowed to have in

Kiss and spitting images: (left to right) Gene, Peter, Ace, Paul

the house. She says I can have a Kiss room. Currently I have a Kiss drape in the front room. I can't see a problem with it, but it's women and relationships, isn't it? You have to compromise. Because I do most of the cooking, I'm allowed to have Kiss posters on the inside of the cupboard doors. We went to stay with my mum in Bristol and she kindly let us have the double bed in her room. It was then that Dawn realised that my mum has two Kiss posters in her bedroom. That's when Dawn saw the gargantuan size of the problem. If anything, Dawn is more of a Wicked Lester fan. When we move in together I'll tone it down and then it'll creep in slowly.

"There is no middle ground with Kiss. You either hate them or you're a Kiss fanatic. You don't just kinda like 'em. It's a sad fact that, as a 38-year-old, the first thing I did when I got Internet access was to go straight to Kiss websites. I have a big Kiss calendar on my wall at work. All my computer passwords are Kiss-related. The first section I go to in a music store is still always Kiss, even though I have everything. What the hell do I expect to find, the lost recordings?"**

"I actually initiated the Kiss reunion. Alex Dickson and I went to South America with Bruce Dickinson. We did three nights in Sao Paolo. On the third night we were told we didn't need to soundcheck, but we told the crew that we weren't happy and we still wanted to soundcheck.

We had this huge empty arena in Sao Paolo. And this is the city where Kiss took the make-up off. Bruce isn't there, of course. We come out in make-up doing 'I Stole Your Love'. The crew were pissing themselves. Okay lads, that was worth getting out of bed for. Bruce turned up halfway through and told us we were sad. But that was the catalyst: we'd put the make-up back on where they'd taken it off. We healed those wounds. And that was 1995. Kiss got the vibe. Shall we do it again?"

Andy Hunns

Design manager of London-based advertising agency Small Japanese Soldier, Andy Hunns wears a double platinum wedding ring inset with a black diamond!

"I was seven when my brother David gave me the first Kiss album in 1975. David is 15 years older than me and he was into Zeppelin and AC/DC. He bought the Kiss album but he didn't like it very much, but he thought I'd like it because I was really into the glam-band Sweet. I would play air drums to Sweet when they were on *Top Of The Pops*. I thought they looked cool, like spacemen. I'd never seen anything like it. Then I bought *Alive!*, which was very exciting because it was my first gatefold album.

"Kiss are larger than life, larger than any band ever. You expect their sound to be bigger than it actually it is, but the songs are fantastic, great pop songs.

"I grew up in Sunderland where we had a rock club called the Mayfair, and there was a guy there who used to dress up as Gene Simmons every Friday night. He had the lot – the make-up, the boots, the cloak – and when they played Kiss songs he did all the moves.

"After the club shut at two o'clock on the Saturday morning, he used to do fire-breathing in the carpark – and every time he did it he was arrested, because the police station was directly opposite the club. The police would just wait for him to start, and then nick him. I wonder where he is now..."

Howard Johnson

Magazine editor, Internet publisher, author and journalist, Howard Johnson was formerly the singer for Brit rockers Dawn After Dark, who, legend has it, went nowhere – and then backwards.

"Geoff Barton at *Sounds* was the guru of all things rock and also the world's greatest Kiss fan. People won't understand this now, but *Sounds* was literally the only place where you could find out anything about rock music. I must have read something of Geoff Barton's in 1978 when I was 14, and Kiss really were larger than life, people from outer space. The first records that came out when I was aware of Kiss were the four solo albums. I remember going into the HMV shop in Manchester with my dinner money, which I'd saved. I never ate anything so I could buy records. I couldn't afford the albums but I bought two singles from the solo albums: Gene Simmons's 'Radioactive', on red vinyl; and Paul Stanley's 'Hold Me, Touch Me', on purple vinyl. I thought it was really cool that they all came out on the same day, but when I listened to them I thought, 'Fucking hell, they're useless!'. 'Hold Me, Touch Me' was limp as a lettuce! But for some reason I decided to give them another chance. I bought *Dynasty* in Manchester's Arndale Centre. I liked the cover, and when I heard the disco song, 'I Was Made For Lovin' You', it was bizarre but I really liked it. So my introduction to Kiss was not of them as a hard rockin' band but as these strange looking people. It all seemed strangely exotic. The make-up was amazing and had a real effect on people of my age. I used to go to a record shop called Yanks, which imported cut-outs from America, and anything American was better than British. The first one I bought was *Love Gun*, and I thought I'd better not show it to my mum and dad because there was all these busty women on the cover – a bit cheeky for a cartoon. When I opened the shrink-wrapping these two things popped out: one was my very own Love Gun, a piece of paper which you could fold up using very detailed instructions that nobody could understand, and eventually you could shake this gun and this thing came out that said, 'Bang!'.

> "Kiss aren't great musicians. The lyrics are naff most of the time. But without sounding too tacky, **they've got spirit. They're hilarious and they know they are.** The reason you love them is more than irony. And they write great pop songs. Paul Stanley is a great pop writer. And they're funny.

And there was also a form to join the Kiss Army. The address was Canooga Park in California, which I thought was so amazing, this whole operation. Even the Aucoin Management logo was cool. You couldn't resist it, whether the music was any cop or not. It was irresistible to young kids who wanted to rock!

"I went to see Kiss at Bingley Hall in 1980. I was very excited and wearing Paul Stanley make-up on the coach from Manchester. I'd just started writing for *Sounds*. Dante Bonutto gave me a present of Kiss make-up. I felt like a complete knob on the coach in my make-up, but I got maximum respect from the other Kiss fans. Looking back, I think what a tool – what a stupid thing to do.

"I saw them in 1983 when I was at university with a mate, Barry Ellis. We went on his horrendous coach to Brussels, city of many canals. We got to know some girls and we had a bit of a laugh. There's a photo of me leaning against a neon sign saying, 'TITS'. Somehow I got backstage to meet them because I worked for *Kerrang!*, and during the gig, Paul Stanley said, 'This is for Howard Johnson'. I thought, 'Fuck me, this is amazing'. I did have a bootleg of the gig but fuck knows what happened to it. After the gig we met them again at the hotel and they were a bit offhand, but getting mentioned by them live on stage was quite exciting.

The best person in the band is Ace Frehley, by a mile. He's the most don't give a fuck-ish of all of them. A guy who clearly was a bit mad and a bit fucked up and a bit of a rocker. He was the funniest. And the story about him wearing two different baseball boots to his audition has always held a place dear in my heart. When I saw him at Bingley Hall he couldn't move, just stayed rooted to the spot and swayed. So hats off to him – he's my kind of rock star. I don't want a man with a briefcase."

Joe Mackett

Managing Editor of UK style magazine **Arena***, Joe Mackett was known in a previous life as "Heavy Metal Joe".*

"I was 14 when I went on holiday to Canada and stayed with relatives. My cousins were all Kiss fans. It was 1979 and everywhere I went Kiss were on the radio. We went out on Halloween and loads of kids were in Kiss make-up. All I'd heard by then was 'I Was Made For Lovin' You', which my sister had. I wanted to see a big stadium rock show when I was there. Kiss played there on the day I

Terrorvision featuring Leigh Marklew, far right

flew home, so I ended up seeing a Canadian band called Trooper at the Enormodome, which was great but it wasn't Kiss. On the day I left the whole town was going Kiss-mad and I sat on the plane thinking, I could have been at a Kiss gig right now.

"I'd heard about Kiss by reading *Sounds*, with Geoff Barton raving about them. Kiss were so big, their show was so extravagant they could never bring it over to the UK. In Canada, I became aware of the Kiss Army, this massive machine. They were so huge and I preferred to champion the underdog with bands like Blackfoot. The only place you could conceive of seeing Kiss was at Donington.

"It was the live albums that got me really into Kiss. Their studio albums weren't the greatest, but *Alive!* and *Alive II* were fantastic. Listening to them, you could image Gene Simmons fire-breathing.

"I loved the music but what really got me was the myth surrounding Kiss. Nobody had ever seen them without the make-up. You'd hear stories that Gene Simmons would go shopping in full make-up. It would be different now, with paparazzi and MTV following bands around all the time, but back then you could believe that Kiss really were aliens! When they finally took the make-up off, I went to a record store just to look at the album cover and see what they really looked like. After that, it was never the same again."

Leigh Marklew

Formerly the bass player with the British rock band Terrorvision.

"My love of – nay, obsession with – Kiss began back in about 1980, when I was 11 years old. At the time The Boomtown Rats didn't have to fight with anyone for poster space on my bedroom wall. However, at around the time the Rats started to lose the plot and began releasing tosh like 'Banana Republic', my older brother, Loz, began his stay at 'big' school. With this came his love of all things heavy metal (the New Wave Of British Heavy Metal, to be precise). We had always loved Queen in our family, but Loz had now started bringing home Motörhead, AC/DC and Saxon records from Discount Records in Keighley, my home town in

Paul Stanley with the world's silliest guitar

'YEEEAAAHHH!' Of course I wanted to fucking buy them! And from that day, my obsession started.

"The following weekend, I begged my folks for an advance on my pocket money and headed off to Discount Records to see if they had any other albums by my new favourite band. I returned home with *Dynasty* and *Unmasked*, which I think had just been released. As I pored over the sleeve to *Unmasked* I listened to the two albums, at first a little confused at some of the poppier stuff, but after three or four spins the effect was complete. I realized that this amazing looking band, who played music that immediately appealed to me, never appeared in public without their unique face paint! I'm sorry Slipknot, Marilyn Manson, Alice Cooper, et al, but you just didn't come close! At 11 years old, without any of my friends knowing about them, Kiss became the coolest band to have all to myself.

"Of course, then the deluge started. The following birthdays and Christmases served solely to complete my entire Kiss collection. And while I was blasting out the albums in my bedroom, I was also adorning the walls with as many Kiss posters, artifacts and other crap as I could find. I soon realized that Woolworths couldn't satisfy my demand, so I started buying *Sounds* magazine and responding to the small ads at the back (anyone remember RS records in Wiveliscombe?) so I could buy posters and singles and all manner of wonderful things that none of my friends had (obviously, by now my friends were all into Kiss as well). I even joined my first (and only) fan club – the Kiss Army (UK Branch). Now this wasn't so wonderful. I seem to remember ordering a silk tour jacket (how stylish!) and never seeing that or my hard earned postal orders again. Still, I didn't hold this against Gene, Paul, Ace or Peter. No, the band could do no wrong in my eyes and the collection steadily grew and grew.

"One of the most exciting times was when Kiss were about to release *The Elder*. This was the first brand new Kiss album I would buy, and it had been delayed and cloaked in mystery for a few months. Little did I know that Ace Frehley was

Yorkshire. But one time, after a day discussing all things rock (and wishing their hair was longer) with his new school friends, he came home with two albums by a band who were little known in the UK – Kiss!

"Robin Milstead (a new-found pal and fellow rocker) was selling these two albums and Loz wondered if I would like them. I looked at the sleeves, drooling. I placed the vinyl on mum and dad's Sanyo stereogram. I placed the headphones on my head. The albums were *Alive II* and *Love Gun*.

more interested in driving his DeLorean on the wrong side of freeways – no doubt suitably refreshed on something from the liquor store – than contributing to an album that he, in fact, hated. I remember Geoff Barton's five-star review in *Sounds* as if it was yesterday, and how this whet my appetite even further. And when I finally got the album I loved it, even though it contained some stuff never heard on a Kiss album before (perhaps that's the echoey sound when you disappear up your own backside?). No, my love never faltered, not through *The Elder* or the much heavier *Creatures Of The Night*, or when Ace Frehley departed and was replaced by that knob-head Vinnie Vincent. I even saw the appeal of the band removing the make up for *Lick It Up*, although when we saw them *au naturel* we all agreed they should put it back on!

"But after more albums that sounded the same as the last, without the make-up or the blood and fire, without the mystique, and to be honest, without the toons, the love affair slowly burned itself out and I contented myself with memories and grainy bootleg footage of the halcyon years of 1974–1980. It was comparable to Terrovision losing their silver suits – the kids just didn't dig it no more!

"At that point I was a huge Status Quo fan. Indeed, a Quo concert at Munster was the first gig I ever attended. **But Kiss were light years away from the denim and three-chord boogie offered by the Quo.** Kiss weren't just mere musicians. They were like Slade, T-Rex and Alice Cooper rolled into one. No, better than that, **they were gargantuan heavy metal rock gods!"**

"So by the early 90s, as I embarked on the search for rock'n'roll Valhalla with my own combo, Kiss had become something of a minor embarrassment to me. There was no way I could persuade the other boys in Terrorvision to cover a Kiss song. Anyway, do you really think Shutty could replicate the Catman's powerhouse-jazz fills and beats? Could Yatesy shoot rockets from his Les Paul? (However, he did have the Ace-patented wobble down pat!) And Tone could never out-camp and out-pout Paul, could he? No, I happily went along with Motörhead and Free and Men At Work covers for the good of inter-band politics.

"We did manage, however, to have ourselves a few Leigh & Lloyd-patented 'Kiss Nights' while travelling the highways and byways of Europe on tour. After a particularly lively tequila session in Hamburg, which ended with the EMI Germany representative leaving the venue splattered in grapes, we boarded the tour bus and, once glasses and noses had been recharged, slotted a Kiss video in the player, turned up the volume and woke up in Denmark the following morning with the bus in pieces, our guitarist with a broken ankle and every-one else with red, blood-stained faces. We stumbled around Copenhagen the next day, searching our mind for clues to the carnage, and finally decided who to blame: Kiss! Lloyd and I acted sheepish for the cameras, but gave each other that knowing look to say, 'We showed 'em everything we got, we kept on dancin' and the bus got hot!'.

"On another occasion it was a dressing room in Milan that took the brunt of a no-holds-barred, full fucking volume Kiss session when the *You Wanted The Best* live album came out during the reunion tour. Apologies to Def Leppard if you got a bill for that!

"Yes, some people may deny a particular fondness for our New York superheroes but they were always the best party-til-you-puke, OTT, gonzoid band to walk this planet (and probably a few others!). And if you disagree with that I'll fight you for it!"

Kiss: hands down, The Hottest Band In The World

Rudy Reed

Manager of Napalm Death and The Wildhearts, Rudy Reed is officially the scruffiest man in the rock business.

"My Saturday afternoons generally consisted of loitering in record shops. One day I was browsing through the 'K' section when I came came across the Holy Grail of live albums, *Alive II*. When I opened up the gatefold sleeve my love affair with Kiss truly began. Flames, make-up, a stage design that blew my adolescent mind! Kiss were my new favourite rock lords: Gene Simmons's God Of Thunder out-fucking Marilyn Manson by a good

twenty years with blood dripping from his painted face; Paul Stanley, a Marc Bolan for the Marvel Comics generation; Ace Frehley, still the coolest head ever to float above planet Earth; and Peter Criss! I'm still not sure what effect Criss had on me, but when my tattoo fixation got the better of me I had a club inked above my left nipple in homage to the Catman!

"I was hooked. I didn't really care that Kiss sounded like Mud, the useless 70's glam band. I asked the guy in the record shop to play me a couple of tracks and, 'You wanted the best . . .' – fuck me, what a start to an album! As the feedback

> "I saw them at the Marquee in 1988 when they were warming up for Donington. And to be that close to Gene's tongue was quite scary. To see one of your favourite bands that close was amazing. **To see Kiss in a club in front of 500 people . . . my friends in America are so jealous of that. They can't get their heads around it."**

eased from 'Detroit Rock City' into 'King Of The Night Time World', I would gladly have bought six copies of *Alive II*!

"Fast forward to 1978 and I'm reading through my music bible *Sounds* when I come across reviews of the four Kiss solo albums. I can still remember leaving Revolver Records in Kettering with all four albums plus The Jam's *All Mod Cons* (another genuine classic) and wondering which one I should play first. After many stoned evenings locked in my bedroom, I finally sequenced my ultimate Kiss album from the four solo records. Paul Stanley came out on top, always the best songwriter in the band. It was inevitable that the Starchild would deliver the best all-round album, with Simmons a close second.

"In 1980 I was outside Stafford Bingley Hall with my mate, Chub. We're prepared to sleep rough tonight. In my wallet I have all my savings and tickets for all of Kiss's UK shows. Then another Kiss fan tells us that the band are staying in a hotel just down the road. We hang around for hours but there is no sign of our heroes. Early next morning I reach into my back pocket for my wallet and it's gone – with all my money and, most importantly, my Kiss tickets. Sweet mother of God, gone! But the Dice Gods are smiling on me. On explaining

my profound distress to a woman who is opening the doors to the venue, she tells me she'll have a word with Kiss's tour manager. As good as her word, she returns with the tour manager and he gives myself and Chub Access All Areas passes! For all the gigs! Thank you, you sick and wonderfully twisted Dice Gods!

"We hang around inside the venue all day as the crew transform the bland cowshed into a space-stage worthy of Kiss. Then, sensory over-load! Diana Ross is standing to my right with a Kiss T-shirt on! Onstage, Paul Stanley is in a top hat and leather jacket – eat your heart out, Slash! Frehley the Space Lord appears in a pink jumpsuit and Simmons stomps around with his truly ridiculous axe-bass. And the small, curly-haired guy I've been talking to for the previous ten minutes is sitting behind the drum kit! It's Kiss with no make-up! Me and Chub are watching them soundcheck next to Diana Ross! Thank you, Dice Gods!"

Dave Reynolds

IT supervisor and rock journalist, Dave Reynolds was once nicknamed "Wiggy" by Status Quo.

"Perhaps it was only logical that I should become a Kiss fan after being exposed to Slade, Sweet, Alice Cooper and T-Rex at an impressionable age in the early 70s. I was living in Germany at the time I got 'Kiss-ed' and *Destroyer* was the first Kiss album I heard. I was fascinated by the cover art, but it wasn't until some time later that I saw a TV broadcast of one of the band's 1977 Japanese shows at the Budokan that I became hooked. At that point I was a huge Status Quo fan. Indeed, a Quo concert at Munster was the first gig I ever attended. But Kiss were light years away from the denim and three-chord boogie offered by the Quo. Kiss weren't just mere musicians. They were like Slade, T-Rex and Alice Cooper rolled into one. No, better than that, they were gargantuan heavy metal rock gods!

And the cool thing was that each Kiss member was so different from the others that you could have your favourite. This was also the appeal the Spice Girls would have in the 1990s, although, er, not quite in the same way as with the hottest band in the world!

"A couple of my school friends, Chris and Andreas (or 'Ace' as he is known to this day!), had also seen the Kiss TV broadcast and we soon became hooked on buying albums, posters, anything on Kiss. This also led us to discovering many other North American hard rock bands – Angel, Van Halen, Starz . . . Hey, Gene discovered Angel and Van Halen, so they must be good. Right?

"Much to the chagrin of the 'beautiful people' in our sixth form, who chose to listen to Supertramp or Madness or the pop music of the day, we formed the King's Kiss Army, named after King's School that we attended. Along with another kid called Mike, I recall performing two Kiss songs dressed up (to the best of our ability at the time) as Kiss at a Christmas School Revue in 1979. I was Paul because I knew the words to the songs we mimed to – 'Detroit Rock City' and 'I Was Made For Lovin' You' – but I looked more like Peter with the cat make-up on. After that, if we had a party I'd dress up like the Catman, and because of that Peter was sort of my favourite member of the band.

"When Kiss announced gigs in Germany in the spring of 1980 we were among the first to grab tickets. However, we were soon gutted to learn that the tour was cancelled and, shock, Peter had left! Was this the end of Kiss? No. They recruited Eric Carr, both a nicer guy and a more talented drummer. But I moved back to England, missing the UK shows and the German gigs, which my mates went to. I was distraught! Still, they got me a programme . . .

"Back in the UK I was able to increase my collection of Kiss memorabilia and began to put together my own Kiss fanzines – purely for my own enjoyment – and joined the short-lived UK arm of the Kiss Army. I remember going to a convention held in a bar under the old Great Western Hotel outside Paddington Station in London in the summer of 1981 and signed a birthday card for Gene, along with everyone else who attended the event. This card is featured in the *Kisstory* book.

"We hang around inside the venue all day as the crew transform the bland cowshed into a space-stage worthy of Kiss. **Then, sensory overload! Diana Ross is standing to my right with a Kiss T-shirt on!** Me and Chub are watching them soundcheck next to **Diana Ross!**"

"In late 1982 Kiss visited the UK for a press tour to promote the newly released *Creatures Of The Night* album and they made a personal appearance at the Virgin Megastore in Oxford Street. I queued outside from around 11am until 4 or 5pm in order to meet the band and get my album signed. There was an amazing atmosphere among the Kiss Army gathered that day, but the mood was rather spoilt by the heavy-handed antics of the police and the security staff.

Still, it was a real eye-opener meeting the band. Gene was great, though a little sarcastic. Eric was very friendly and commented on the Gene jumper I was wearing that my mother had made for me a few years earlier. Ace was noticeably drunk and actually fell over after he'd signed my record. And Paul was a complete prick! I asked him a question and he completely ignored me. I was so disgusted I went home and removed all the posters I had of him (including a now quite rare solo album poster) and later gave them all to Kevin Kozak of the Mancunian glam band Rox.

"Paul's rudeness stuck with me for years, even up to the point where I was regularly interviewing the band for *Kerrang!* I have always found Gene friendlier, though terribly superior in his attitude. He has this annoying habit of mimicking English accents, but always ends up sounding like a very bad Dick Van Dyke in *Mary Poppins*.

"I used to work part-time in Shades, the now-legendary hard rock import specialists in Central London, and Gene and Paul came in near to closing time one Saturday evening. This was just after the *Asylum* album had been released. Gene wanted to buy some French magazines and I am convinced to this day that somehow I managed to short-change him!

"Although the *Lick It Up* album was a fairly decent record, the fact that the make-up had come off led me to decide that Kiss were now a fairly ordinary band and prompted me not to bother going to see them play at any of the UK gigs in the autumn of 1983. In fact, I didn't get to see Kiss live until 1988 when they appeared on the bill below Iron Maiden at the Monsters Of Rock event at Donington that year.

"Simmons was up to his old tricks backstage at that gig. My girlfriend Nikki, a gorgeous petite blonde and the love of my life, asked for his autograph and opened her jacket wanting him to sign her pass. Of course, Simmons thought she wanted him to sign her breasts – until he was promptly told otherwise!

"I had actually seen Kiss a few weeks prior to the event, albeit Gene and Paul making a very special appearance for the encore of a Frehley's Comet show at the Limelight in New York City. They played 'Deuce'. It was the first time the trio had appeared on stage together since the promo tour for *Creatures Of The Night* in 1982. It was awesome. Members of Anthrax were down the front and in heaven. Earlier that day Kiss had been hanging around backstage at the Monsters Of Rock show headlined by Van Halen at the Giants Stadium across the Hudson River in New Jersey. I always remember Eric Carr following these girls around – real lookers – who were in a band, only for one of them to make him look really stupid in front of everybody by asking him if he was going to keep following them around like a little dog all day. When told this story at an interview the next day Gene found it very amusing.

"Eric Carr's death was a terrible tragedy, and I think it really shocked a great many Kiss fans, including myself. He was one hell of a drummer and a really genuine guy who, sadly, I never had the chance to interview.

"The reunion of the original band in 1996 was greeted with excitement and cynicism. We all knew they were doing it for the money and felt extremely sorry for Bruce Kulick and Eric Singer, but the chance to see the original band back in make-up and with the promise of the full, fire and brimstone show was just too good to miss. Despite feeling rather disappointed with the Donington show they played that summer, the Wembley concert later that year was out of this world. They were simply fantastic. Maybe it's time for Kiss to call it a day, but many thanks for the memories!"

Bruce Kulick gets his leg over Paul Stanley

Bon Jovi: booed by Kiss fan Graham Stroud!

Graham Stroud

Insurance broker Graham Stroud accompanied the author on his first trip to a Kiss gig, in 1984.

"Around 1981 a friend and I were fighting over two albums in a second-hand record shop. In the end, he got *Alive II* and I got Aerosmith's *Live Bootleg*, which was no bad thing, but we both wanted *Alive II* because it was on blood-red vinyl. Because of this I had this downer on Kiss, and the next time I came across them was when a new girl started at school. She was gorgeous, and she had a Kiss badge on her jacket. I tried it on and was rejected, so that was the second reason I hated Kiss. She wasn't a rock chick at all. I think she got into them via her brother. I felt let down by Kiss.

"The first time I really liked them was when I saw the video for 'I Love It Loud'. I thought, 'Wow, what a great band!' When I went to college I met up with a few other Kiss maniacs. Back then, friendships were formed purely on the basis of whether you were into heavy metal. A friend taped me *Creatures Of The Night*, which I loved, and just after that *Lick It Up* came out.

Up to that point none of my friends wanted to see Kiss live, but when *Animalize* was released in 1984 we all went to Wembley Arena. Bon Jovi opened and they were terrible. Jon Bon Jovi came on draped in an American flag, so I stood on my seat and booed him. Then Kiss came on and Eric Carr was in a tank that fired missiles into the crowd, and Paul Stanley lost his microphone when he was swinging it round his head. It went flying off into row W!

I remember Paul doing a Marcel Marceau impersonation – not saying a word but splitting the crowd into two and getting them to shout. They also did a bizarre rendition of 'La Bamba' followed by 'Winchester Cathedral'! What the fuck was that all about? For the whole gig I couldn't keep my eyes off Paul Stanley.

"I actually went to America to see Kiss many years later. I'd seen the reunion tour and also the 3-D extravaganza. The funny thing about the 3-D show was that the only songs I remember having 3-D effects were the new songs, which were terrible. At least it took my mind off the music. When Kiss did the farewell tour, I flew out to visit a friend in Boston. There was no guarantee that the tour would come to Europe. We had a 90-minute road trip to get the gig in Mansfield, Massacusetts, and it was horrible – mullet city! It was a bizarre line-up. First on were Skid Row, without Sebastian Bach. We only saw the last song and it was truly horrendous. Then it was Ted Nugent. I walked out after three songs when he did a rant saying, 'If you can't speak American, fuck off out of our country,' or something like that. Then Kiss came on.

"Eight of us went, and I'd only met one of them before. A couple of them were really cliquey, but there was one point when this arrogant sod called Fat Boy Dave, who hadn't spoken to me all day, suddenly turned to me when Kiss started up 'Heaven's On Fire', and we both went, 'Whoah-oh-oh-oh-oh!', gave each other the metal sign, and an instant friendship was formed. It was a great gig. Well, it was exactly the same as every other Kiss gig, but because it was the farewell tour, it was very emotional. There were tears in our eyes. Tears were falling! It's romance, isn't it? It's my band. I was the only English person there. Everybody else had grown up listening to the band from a very early age, but I felt just as emotional because I realised I was never going to see this band again.

"Kiss are one of the few bands I'm happy to see purely on a nostalgia trip. With anyone else I want new songs, but I want to see Kiss stuck firmly in the late 70s. They haven't done a good album in years, have they? Nobody goes to see the new stuff and Kiss know that, although on that farewell tour they were doing 'Heaven's On Fire' and 'Tears Are Falling' with Ace and Peter in the band, which was weird. It was a greatest hits show. Gene is a businessman first and rock star second, and he knows what his punters want. He knows that if Kiss turned up and played a load of songs off the last couple of albums, they wouldn't fill the stadiums. They were charging a lot of money for tickets. I paid $75 to see them, which is obscene. Plus £200 for a plane ticket. But it was worth it. I didn't really have enough money to go, but it was Kiss.

"They were even great live without the make-up. On the *Hot In The Shade* tour they had a big black curtain over the front of the stage, in true Kiss tradition. The lights went down, the curtain came down, and there was an enormous sphinx's head with laser eyes. The mouth dropped and the four members of the band came out waving at the crowd, returning heroes. That's what you want: spectacle. They always put on a show, but I saw them at the Marquee in 1988 when they were warming up for Donington. It was the opening night of the new Marquee in Charing Cross Road. People have slagged Kiss for not being a great live band but at the Marquee they were great. They could only just get the drum kit on the stage. And to be that close to Gene's tongue was quite scary. To see one of your favourite bands that close was amazing. Nowadays you have Oasis playing an intimate show at Shepherds Bush Empire in front of two or three thousand people, but to see Kiss in a club in front of 500 people . . . my friends in

"Eight of us went, and I'd only met one of them before. A couple of them were really cliquey, but there was one point when this arrogant sod called Fat Boy Dave, who hadn't spoken to me all day, **suddenly turned to me when Kiss started up 'Heaven's On Fire', and we both went, 'Whoah-oh-oh-oh-oh!',** gave each other the metal sign, and an instant friendship was formed."

America are so jealous of that. They can't get their heads around it. The live show is the most important thing to me and the reunion show at Wembley Arena was the best Kiss show I've ever seen. Pure 1976. Phenomenal.

"Kiss aren't great musicians. The lyrics are naff most of the time. But without sounding too tacky, they've got spirit. They're hilarious and they know they are. The reason you love them is more than irony. And they write great pop songs. Paul Stanley is a great pop writer. And they're funny.

"A very good friend of mine in the States, Jason Loeb, got married to a girl whose maiden name is Andrea Stanley. She was expecting their first baby and there's a tradition in the family that if the child is a boy, the middle name is Stanley. Jason convinced her to call the baby Paul. He phoned me one night and said, 'She's agreed', and I knew exactly what he was talking about. A day later they were sitting at home watching TV and she looked at him and said, 'No!'. He said, 'What are you talking about?', and she says, 'Paul Stanley – no!'."

Mark Taylor

Mark Taylor lives in Glasgow with his long-suffering wife, Fiona.

"There is no middle ground with Kiss. You either hate them or you're a Kiss fanatic. You don't just kinda like 'em. It's a sad fact that, as a 38-year-old, the first thing I did when I got Internet access was go straight to Kiss websites. I have a big Kiss calendar on my wall at work. All my computer passwords are Kiss-related. The first section I go to in a music store is still always Kiss, even though I

have everything. What the hell do I expect to find, the lost recordings?

"I was a late starter with Kiss. My college mate got me into them in 1982. I was a mad Alice Cooper fan and he loaned me *Alive II*. 'Detroit Rock City' just blew me away. It was better than my first sexual encounter – and that was only a year earlier! Being a poor student, I had no money and would walk the eight miles to my friend's house to listen to the Kiss album of the week. In 1983 Kiss announced a tour so two heavy metal 'numpties' decided to camp out all night for tickets. We were well-prepared: six pints in the pub, tight jeans, baseball boots, sleeveless T-shirts . . . it's a miracle we didn't catch hypothermia!

"The gig was amazing and we went to the Albany Hotel in Glasgow the following day to try to meet the band. Paul Stanley appeared and I thought my chest was going to explode with excitement, but the best bit was meeting Gene. My friend Peter was so nervous he came out with the classic line, 'What did you have for breakfast?' 'Eggs, my friend,' Gene replied. Not knowing what to say next, Peter said, 'How did you have your eggs done?'. 'Scrambled,' was the reply. Peter had wanted to ask Gene if he's had a traditional Scottish breakfast but just couldn't get the words out straight!

"While Kiss were playing in Glasgow a local cinema was screening *Kiss Meets The Phantom Of The Park*, so after meeting the band I went to see the movie for the fourth time and took my camera. What a sad, sad boy I was, taking pictures of the cinema screen because Kiss were on it!

"In 1984 I went to Wembley Arena and asked if there were any tickets left for the Kiss show that night. The woman in the box office asked us if the front row was alright! We caught loads of plectrums which were later made into earrings, which I still have to this day!

"There was also a shop in Carnaby Street that had a brilliant poster of Gene on the wall. For four years, every time I visited London I'd go to the shop and ask if I could buy the poster but they'd never agree to sell it. Eventually the green-eyed monster got the better of me and I nicked it off the

Paul Stanley can make a grown man cry

The band's first album, simply titled *Kiss*, was released on February 18, 1974 through Neil Bogart's fledgling label Casablanca, which would become synonymous with the flamboyance and excess of the disco era through hit records by Donna Summer, the Village People and Cher.

3 THE 1970s

KISS

Kiss was met with indifference by critics (setting a precedent for the band's entire career), but it is now acknowledged as one of the classic hard rock debuts. Kiss features several songs that Paul Stanley and Gene Simmons had written for their previous band, Wicked Lester, and many of the ten tracks have remained staples of the Kiss live show for three decades: "Strutter", "Firehouse", "Deuce", "Cold Gin" and "Black Diamond".

The album cover was shot by celebrated rock photographer Joel Brodsky, whose previous work included The Doors's *Strange Days* and several outrageous covers for funk maestros the Ohio Players. Brodsky hired a make-up artist for the shoot, hence Peter Criss's make-up appears different from the green-hued cat mask known and loved by Kiss fans.

■ Strutter

For any rock 'n' roll band, the first song on the first album is a mission statement: a song in which the group's sound is immediately and powerfully defined. To kick off their debut, Kiss chose "Strutter", written by Paul Stanley and Gene Simmons yet indelibly stamped with Stanley's out-sized charisma. As an introduction to the bawdy, larger-than-life rock'n'roll that would be Kiss's trademark over the ensuing thirty years, "Strutter" is perfect. The formula is classically simple: a thumping backbeat, a wholly appropriate strutting riff with neat interplay between Paul Stanley and Ace Frehley, a couple of verses in which a pouting Paul gossips about a prickteasing woman, an urgent bridge leading to a crudely effective chorus chanted over a second riff even better than the first, an explosive solo from Ace and an emphatic powerchord to finish. In a little over three minutes, Kiss had arrived as the most exciting new rock band in America. For years Kiss would be derided as a circus act of negligible musical worth, yet from the very first song on their debut album, Kiss were creating classic rock anthems.

Andy Hunns: "I nearly creamed myself when they opened with 'Strutter' at Donington in 1988. I couldn't believe it. Everybody was expecting Kiss to fall flat on their arses because they didn't have the make-up, but they did a classic show. I was fearing the worst but they only did one song post-'84. And when they opened up with 'Strutter' I was just in heaven. It's the best Kiss song, in my mind. It's got everything: the pop; the dark side to it; and a great hook. My favourite Kiss song changes all the time, but 'Strutter' is the one I always come back to."

Graham Stroud: "It's not just a great Kiss song; it's a classic rock song."

Paul Stanley - The Starchild

■ Nothin' To Lose

Having established their hard rock credentials in emphatic style with "Strutter", Kiss showed off their pop nous with "Nothin' To Lose", the first single to be lifted from the album. If anything, this tune proved that Kiss had the brass balls to try any style of music that took their fancy. Written by Gene Simmons, "Nothin' To Lose" begins with the kind of mean, bass-driven riff that would become Simmons' stock in trade, but within just a few bars the mood lightens as Kiss fool around with one of their most playful pop arrangements. Gene and Paul sing the verses but it's Peter Criss who leads the chorus, delivered with a dash of old-fashioned doo-wop style, handclaps, boogie-woogie piano and all. As Peter ad-libs and whoops and laughs, his Italian-American New Yorker accent is unmistakable. Kiss have always made feelgood music, but never have they sounded more like they're having fun than on "Nothin' To Lose".

Dave Reynolds: "I love this track because it not only features Paul and Gene on vocals, but they managed to persuade the Catman to provide some very neat ad-libs in the chorus. A typically 70s rock'n'roll song with a hint of 50s shake, rattle and roll. You hardly notice the piano on the studio version!"

■ Firehouse

What Gene Simmons describes as an "audio-visual" experience has been the key to Kiss's success, and from the group's inception they wrote songs geared to their over-the-top stageshow. Paul Stanley's "Firehouse" is a classic example: presenting opportunities for Paul to wear a comical fireman's hat and for Gene to demonstrate his fire-breathing skills, which he learnt from a magician at the behest of manager Bill Aucoin.

Somebody, Aucoin told the group, is going to breathe fire onstage, and while Paul, Ace and Peter stood motionless, Gene volunteered. His confidence backfired when Kiss played at New York's Academy of Music on New Year's Eve, 1973. Wanting to look "extra cool" for such a high-profile gig, Simmons had used rather more hairspray than usual, which resulted in his hair catching fire. As Simmons smelled burning, an alert roadie rushed onstage and wrapped his flaming head in a wet towel. The crowd, needless to say, went wild.

"Firehouse" would remain a showpiece in the Kiss live set for the next thirty years – and the song itself is no mere novelty tune. Built on a slow, funky riff, it features more of the band's clever multi-lead vocal work and a comical refrain of "Woo-ooh yeah!", plus, of course, the inevitable wailing of a fire-engine siren.

Andy Hunns: "I love what happens during that song. Gene does his bit, Paul does his bit; it's a massive group song. I came so close to getting Paul Stanley's fireman's helmet at Newcastle City Hall in 1983. When he threw it I touched it, I had my hand on it, but it was snatched away from me."

Mark Taylor: "When Kiss played Glasgow in 1974 my friend Peter and I had a big plan to get Paul Stanley's firehat when they played "Firehouse". When Paul threw the hat, Peter would cup his hands and vault me into the air where I would catch it. Voila! Only one problem: they did-n't play "Firehouse". Great song, though. It just makes your groin thrust!"

■ Cold Gin

A blast of pure hard rock dynamics, "Cold Gin" boasts the best riff on the first Kiss album; hardly surprising given that its author is guitarist Ace Frehley. Gene Simmons sings lead vocal after Paul has yelled "Whooh!" and "Alright!", but the song is a typical Ace Frehley rocker: a tough tale of street-corner alcoholism set to some gritty heavy metal riffing.

Joe Mackett: "When you're 18 and you've just started drinking properly, 'Cold Gin' makes you want to go out and try some – and then you realise it's disgusting! It's a bit like Riot's 'Swords And Tequila'."

Andy Hunns: "I love the bit at the end when Ace, Paul and Gene line up onstage. When you're 11 years old and you're watching Kiss, it's just the biggest thing you've ever seen, and when they did

Kevin Keegan, England football hero and Kiss fan

the moves in 'Cold Gin' it was so cool. That was what made me want to be in a band. Then I looked over and saw Kevin Keegan and the England squad standing there in suits. They were playing Northern Ireland at Wembley the night after and they were all there."

Graham Stroud: "The introduction to 'Cold Gin' on *Alive!* is the best and worst intro to a song you've ever heard. I did indeed go into pubs in the suburbs and confidently order a cold gin, only to be told that I was too young to be drinking. We drank neat gin with ice just so that if somebody asked what it was, we could say 'Cold gin!'. Three glasses clink together with a shout of, 'It's cold gin time again!'"

■ Let Me Know

Like "Nothin' To Lose", "Let Me Know" is Kiss at their most light-hearted; an old-fashioned, good-time rock'n'roll tune on which Gene and Paul trade verses about Sunday drivers and bundles of joy. For all its cheesiness, "Let Me Know" features some of Gene and Paul's most versatile and heartfelt singing – and there's a surprise in store at the finish when another doo-wop harmony leads to an

Kiss in their 70s pomp: Gene Simmons, Ace Frehley, Paul Stanley

Aerosmith-styled hard rock riff.

Leigh Marklew: "A less popular song off the first album, but it's easier to get tired of 'Cold Gin' and 'Strutter' and 'Firehouse' because we hear them all the time. This simple rock 'n' roll boy-meets-girl offering sums up all that is best about early Kiss. Simplicity, melody, Gene and Paul interchanging vocals. It just rocks – especially the bit where Paul comes in and just rips, 'Did ya ever want lovin'?!'."

■ Kissin' Time

A novelty song recorded by Kiss at the behest of manager Bill Aucoin and label boss Neil Bogart, "Kissin' Time" is the only track on the debut album that was not written by the band. Kiss were never truly comfortable with the song, but it was released as a single and gave Casablanca's promotion staff a hook for publicity stunts, including radio-sponsored kissing competitions.

The song's simple chant namechecks a host of American cities in the style of Martha & The Vandellas's Motown smash "Dancing In The Street". It was a trick that Kiss would rework two years later for their anthem "Detroit Rock City".

■ Deuce

Written by Gene Simmons, "Deuce" is the song with which Kiss opened their early shows in explosive fashion. With Simmons exhorting, "Get up! And get your grandma out of here!", "Deuce" is an urgent, high-energy hard rock anthem which, coupled with Kiss's cartoonish image, stunned audiences when the band supported a variety of big-name rock acts on their first nationwide American tour.

Andy Hunns: "It was the first song I clung on to when I bought *Alive!*. It's a great show-opener but, of course, it was replaced by an even better show-opener in 'Detroit Rock City'."

Leigh Marklew: "It is one of my fave Kiss songs of all time. It is my ambition to one day don full Simmons costume and make-up and perform this with a tribute band! And I love Mr Frehley's rippin' solo."

Dave Reynolds: "The opening line is a classic, and 'Deuce' is one of those songs you can't help

■ Love Theme From Kiss

Certainly the weirdest track on the first album and arguably the strangest song the group have ever recorded, "Love Theme From Kiss" is a slow, low-key instrumental and the only track on the first album composed by all four band members. Befitting a hokey Hollywood title, this unexpected mood piece is delivered in a totally exaggerated corny style.

In the 90s, "Love Theme From Kiss" would be recorded by the Melvins, one of the most influential if wilfully unsuccessful grunge bands who originated from Kurt Cobain's hometown of Aberdeen, Washington. Indeed, Cobain served as a Melvins roadie before forming Nirvana and played drums with the Melvins on a Kiss tribute album. The Melvins paid a further homage to Kiss when they recorded three solo albums in the style of the Kiss solo albums of 1978, complete with replica artwork.

As noted by Phil Alexander, managing editor of the UK's biggest-selling rock title *Kerrang!*, without the Melvins there would have been no Nirvana. And without Kiss, there would be no Melvins. Ergo, no Kiss, no Nirvana. Strange but true. Hence "Love Theme From Kiss" holds a special place in Kiss folklore.

■ 100,000 Years

Beginning with a teasing bass riff from Gene Simmons, "100,000 Years" is one of the most dynamic of early Kiss songs, more complex in structure than, say, "Deuce" or "Strutter", yet no less anthemic. Ace Frehley contributes fiery solos and Paul Stanley sings as if he's already performing before a sold-out stadium.

So many rock albums trail off towards the end after all the good songs are loaded up at the start. Not so Kiss. With "100,000 Years", a joint effort from Simmons and Stanley, the energy goes up another notch.

Andy Hunns: "It's a menacing song. Like 'Black Diamond', it's quite sinister. '100,000 Years' was

The Melvins covered Kiss songs, with Kurt Cobain on drums!

but get up and sing along to."

Chris Dale: "It is the ultimate Kiss rocker. I can't help going a bit mental when they play this one live. I still get really excited like a child before Kiss gigs. I can't stand still, must be down the front and I can't stop giggling before they come on. It never happens with any other band."

Gary Banton: "As soon as Gene does that bass slide off of Paul's intro, you know they mean business! What follows is an unrelenting barrage of riffs that really come from the balls! The pure energy of 'Deuce' makes it my all-time fave Kiss song."

my favourite Kiss song for a long time."

Dave Reynolds: "Simply awesome. Gene's haunting bass intro and pumping rhythm standing out in my mind alongside a very spacey, laid-back feel to the guitar work from Ace. Live, this was another one of those tracks on which Kiss stepped up a few gears. The version on *Alive!* is mind-blowing, with a Criss drum solo and a mid-section that allowed Stanley to involve the crowd big-time. Er, do you mind if I sit down for a while? I need to reacquaint myself with its style!"

■ Black Diamond

To wrap up their debut, Kiss deliver their first epic track. "Black Diamond" starts with a brief passage of acoustic guitar and a gentle vocal from the song's author, Paul Stanley. Then, as Peter Criss clicks his drumsticks, Stanley cries "Hit it!", cueing another powerhouse rock riff.

Criss takes up lead vocals, his streetwise nuances perfectly suiting a tale of hard day-to-day struggle. And there is a surprise ending: a series of Who-inspired powerchords slowing to a breathtaking, head-spinning climax; an emphatic conclusion to a classic first album.

Andy Hunns: "I have a black diamond in my wedding ring and the ring itself is made of double platinum. When we were choosing our wedding rings I liked a certain kind of ring and when they said it was double platinum I thought, 'Fantastic'. Immediately I started thinking of Kiss. The jeweller said, 'Do you want a stone put in it?,' and my wife said, 'Why don't you have a black diamond?' I got very excited and she looked at me and asked me what I was so excited about. I said, 'Kiss!'. As for the song 'Black Diamond', I love the bit at the end when they all go on the platform. It's a great song lyrically, too."

Graham Stroud: "I've got a version by The Replacements on their album *Let It Be*. It's a really good version but it's really straight, there's no messing around on it. With that song, Kiss is the link between my getting out of my metal years and getting into the music I like now. If you ask any of the US rock bands, they're all massive Kiss

Paul, Ace, Peter, Gene: they came from outer space

Anthrax introduced Kiss music to a new generation of rock fans in the 1980s with a cover of the classic "Parasite"

fans. Paul Westerberg from The Replacements was brought up on Kiss. It's American radio rock."

Howard Johnson: "It is everything I don't like about Kiss – a crunching, neanderthal heavy metal song – but the amount of bombs that are let off at the end, you just can't fault it. It's so gumby in its over-the-top-ness. I really warmed to that song because it was the antithesis of everything that people told me I should like."

Dante Bonutto: "With the bombs it was very, very good indeed. Just for the way they went off in all the right places. As a set-closer it's just fantastic."

Chris Dale: "I've got a mate, a big scary skinhead, who literally cries when Kiss play 'Black Diamond' live."

Gary Banton: "Paul's finger-picked intro lulls you into a false sense of security, but you know something big is coming as soon as Peter counts the riff in by clicking his sticks. Peter's voice sounds great on this, nice and raspy with a real r&b edge, and to this day I find the sound of those detuning power chords in the outro to be some of the most dark and sorrowful sounds I've ever heard. Chilling!"

HOTTER THAN HELL

Following a marathon eight-month tour in support of their first album, Kiss headed to Los Angeles to record their second. With production team Richie

Wise and Kenny Kerner again at the helm, *Hotter Than Hell* was cut at the Los Angeles Village Recorder studios, and boasts a raw sound heavier than that of the debut.

Released just eight months after the first album on October 22, 1974, *Hotter Than Hell* also refined the group's image with a stunning cover designed by noted photographer Norman Seeff and based on Japanese kabuki theatre.

■ Got To Choose

Where Kiss's debut kicked off with the uptempo "Strutter", "Got To Choose" makes a different kind of impression, as if the band were intent on proving they had the street smarts to back up their flashy showmanship. Typically of a Paul Stanley composition, the band's characteristic swagger is very much in evidence, but where "Strutter" demanded the listener's attention, "Got To Choose" moved at a slower pace and gave off the heavy aura which pervades much of Hotter Than Hell; a small irony given that Kiss had forsaken New York City for the sunnier climes of California to make the record.

Dave Reynolds: "Kiss always seemed to open their albums with extremely strong songs and this is no exception."

■ Parasite

One of the hardest-hitting songs in the Kiss catalogue, "Parasite" is a thundering, no-frills heavy metal number written by Ace Frehley and sung menacingly by Gene Simmons. In the 1990s the song was covered by Anthrax, the New York group whose high-speed thrash metal helped revolutionize heavy music in the '80s. Anthrax guitarist Scott Ian was a teenage Kiss fanatic who paid his respects with his group's faithful reading of "Parasite".

Dave Reynolds: "Such an evil riff! Possibly the heaviest, nastiest thing Kiss ever recorded."

■ Goin' Blind

"I'm 93, you're 16," Gene Simmons sings on this most unorthodox love song, which the bassist wrote with Stephen Coronel, a longtime friend and bandmate who stood alongside Simmons and Paul Stanley in their pre-Kiss outfit Wicked Lester and played on that band's unreleased album in 1972. As one of rock's most renowned lotharios with an eye for the younger ladies, Simmons effectively wrote his own epitaph with this tragic and somewhat sinister lament.

Like the bizarre "Love Theme From Kiss", "Goin' Blind" was later recorded by seminal grunge band the Melvins on their 1993 album *Houdini*. Astonishingly, the guest drummer on this recording is none other than Kurt Cobain, the Melvins's close friend and former roadie.

Mark Taylor: "A brilliant song that conjures up images of feverish masturbation!"

Howard Johnson: "For a song you expect to be about getting the clap, it's a very soft song. Of course it's about an old man who is literally going

Kurt Cobain - or is it Peter Criss?

Nice boots, Gene!

blind, but in my fevered imagination, he'd got some terrible venereal disease. I thought it was divine retribution for fucking some young girl."

Leigh Marklew: "One thing often overlooked about Gene Simmons is his great sense of melody, heavily Beatles-influenced, no doubt. Here it shines through. A totally brilliant and original toon."

Gary Banton: "A very different tune to the norm! It has an obvious Beatles influence and I've always found the music and lyric to be quite haunting. Ace's solo on this is one of his best. He really seems to wring the pain out of every note he bends here."

■ Hotter Than Hell

If the first three songs on *Hotter Than Hell* differed

radically from the Kiss of the first album, this title track was business as usual: a high-volume, low-IQ rock anthem to which writer Paul Stanley could pout, preen and wiggle his butt. Undoubtedly the most immediate and accessible track on the album.

■ Let Me Go, Rock'n'Roll

As its title implies, "Let Me Go, Rock'n'Roll" is a knockabout party tune, similar both in its name and in its throwaway nature to "Let Me Know" that featured on the band's debut album'. Banged out in a little over two minutes after Gene Simmons has howled "Rock'n'roll!" in the manner of puppet on a children's television show, this

Simmons/Stanley track involves some great lead playing from Ace.

■ All The Way

One of the lesser-known tracks in Kiss history, "All The Way" has Gene Simmons in surly mood and warning a nagging girlfriend: "One of these days you'll push me all the way!". The song is built on a heavy staccato riff featuring Peter Criss bashing a cowbell and bringing some much-needed levity to one of Simmons's more forgettable numbers.

■ Watchin' You

Another Gene Simmons track – but if the preceding "All The Way" is merely functional, "Watchin' You" is one of Gene's best, a powerful, ominous yet grooving heavy rock song on which the band get as close as they've ever done to jamming on record. Before "God Of Thunder", "Watchin' You" was the signature song for Simmons' menacing Demon persona.

Leigh Marklew: "This guttural, rumbling and riff-tastic rocker pretty much sums up Gene Simmons's whole fire-breathing, blood-dribbling Demon persona. Oh, to have been a 13 year-old American when this came out in 1974!"

Dave Reynolds: "A monster metal number that stomps along like Godzilla tearing up everything in his path. Gene spits out the lead vocal with venom. Criss's percussive work and the seemingly never-ending lead play of Ace Frehley prove that, on their day, Kiss were beyond compare. It's interesting to note that Simmons admitted to 're-arranging' the guitar lick from Mountain's 'Mississippi Queen' when writing this track."

■ Mainline

Although written by Paul Stanley, "Mainline" is sung by Peter Criss and has all the hallmarks of the drummer's own pop-rock songs. Again, Criss proves himself a more than capable vocalist, even when he's tackling the frankly ridiculous couplet: "I'm needing some lovin', I'm hot like an oven".

These lines would be reversed by Marvin Gaye on 1982's "Sexual Healing", although it seems unlikely that the troubled soul genius spent much time checking out obscure Kiss album tracks.

Marvin Gaye is hot like an oven
Below, Slade's Noddy Holder enjoys a nice kipper tie

■ Comin' Home

Gene Simmons has frequently cited British glam-rock stars Slade as a major inspiration for Kiss, and nowhere is this more evident than on "Comin' Home", which features a riff uncannily reminiscent of Slade's seasonal 1973 chart-topper "Merry Xmas Everybody". In his autobiography Kiss And Make Up, Simmons mistakenly states that Slade's Walsall-born frontman Noddy Holder is Welsh, but on this Stanley/Frehley track, it is clear that Kiss paid close attention to Slade's populist music. Nevertheless, "Comin' Home" is arguably the best song on *Hotter Than Hell*, and its theme of a touring rock star pining for his girlfriend, while difficult to believe coming from a member of Kiss, would be reprised on Peter Criss's "Beth".

Jimi Hendrix: Kiss cut **Dressed To Kill** *at the studio where Hendrix created his masterpiece* **Electric Ladyland**

■ Strange Ways

Just as *Hotter Than Hell* begins in more muted fashion than the first album, so it lacks the spectacular finish of a song like "Black Diamond". "Strange Ways", *Hotter Than Hell*'s closing track, is in keeping with the album's raw rock style, but following "Comin' Home" it sounds leaden. Of principal interest is the song's lyric, in which Ace Frehley writes of paranoia and isolation. This, coupled with the alcoholic "Cold Gin", pointed to the guitarist's own personal struggle.

Chris Dale: "*Hotter Than Hell* has always been one of my favourite albums. Is it me, or did grunge start with this album? 'Strange Ways', for me, is the forerunner to grunge. Funny how Kiss later tried going grunge on *Carnival Of Souls* and totally missed the point even though they started it all!"

DRESSED TO KILL

Disappointed by sales of the first two Kiss albums, Casablanca boss Neil Bogart urged the group to get back into the studio quickly to capitalise on their fast-growing reputation as the most exciting live rock act in America. Recording at New York's legendary Electric Lady studio, where Jimi Hendrix had cut the awesome *Electric Ladyland*, Kiss locked themselves away to write new songs as fast as they could. Having been on the road constantly since the release of the first album just a year previously, they were in desperate need of new material, but Kiss performed heroically under pressure. Bogart, who co-produced *Dressed To Kill* with the band, demanded a radio-friendly single and Simmons and Stanley responded with "Rock And Roll All Nite", which would become the ultimate Kiss anthem. Brighter and more pop-oriented than *Hotter Than Hell*, *Dressed To Kill* was released on March 19, 1975, and soon after "Rock And Roll All Nite" gave Kiss their first – albeit modest – chart hit.

For the album cover, the band members borrowed suits to pose on a New York street corner: a comical yet iconic image.

■ Room Service

As befits a band who had been touring virtually non-stop for a year, "Room Service" is a classic on-the-road tale in which author Paul Stanley exclaims: "A hotel all alone is not a rock'n'roll star's dream". No matter, there were plenty of willing bedmates across the length and breadth of America, and on the rollicking "Room Service" Stanley revels in his lady-pleasing reputation, detailing his own unique brand of in-room entertainment.

Howard Johnson: "It's a great little rock'n'roll track, really tinny production, cardboard boxes for drums and really bad playing. They can barely keep the tune together. Having been in a band myself which, as someone said, went absolutely nowhere and then backwards, even I know that this is poor playing. It has a certain loose charm, I suppose. It has much more affinity with traditional 50s rock than with heavy metal. And I really like the suits they wore. Gene Simmons, to his credit, had a really great pair of white clogs on. At the time, I thought white clogs was where it was at. Thank fuck I couldn't find any in Manchester."

■ Two Timer

If "Room Service" is pure Paul Stanley, "Two Timer" is all Gene Simmons: a heavy, slow-moving number in which a wounded Simmons berates an unfaithful lover; somewhat ironically, given Simmons's loudly proclaimed motto: "Fuck anything that moves".

■ Ladies In Waiting

Any sympathy that might be aroused by "Two Timer" is immediately crushed by Gene Simmons' next composition, "Ladies In Waiting", in which said ladies are likened to "meat" on a market stall. This is the Gene Simmons of popular folklore: a shameless old womaniser with a ready eye for a politically-incorrect double entendre.

■ Getaway

Written by Ace Frehley and sung by Peter Criss, "Getaway" is a freewheeling, feelgood rock'n'roll number that sounds like it was composed and recorded in a matter of minutes and is all the better for it. The spontaneity of songs like this give *Dressed To Kill* a freshness lacking on *Hotter Than Hell*.

■ Rock Bottom

Echoing the first album's "Black Diamond", Stanley and Frehley's "Rock Bottom" begins with a lovely acoustic prelude before switching to an electrifying, kick-ass riff. Paul Stanley, who wrote the song with Ace Frehley, delivers this hard-knock story with one of his gutsiest performances, guaranteeing instant classic status.

■ C'mon Love Me

If "Room Service" offered a tantalising glimpse of a rock star's life on the road, "C'mon And Love Me" also celebrated the fringe benefits of stardom as writer Paul Stanley tells of a conquest who came on to him after seeing his picture in a music magazine. Needless to say, Stanley and his new admirer waste no time in getting down to business. "C'mon And Love Me" was covered by 80s rock superstars Skid Row.

Andy Hunns: "Brilliant lyrics: 'You were distant, now you're nearer, I can see your face inside the mirror'. Only Paul Stanley could rhyme like that."

Dante Bonutto: "From the moment I first heard this song I thought it was brilliant. I even love the lyrics, although they're a bit corny."

■ Anything For My Baby

A throwback to the pop rock'n'roll of "Let Me Know", this Paul Stanley tune is lightweight, but the band have fun with it, not least Peter Criss, who rattles his kit like a teenager throughout the chorus and sounds like he's warming up for "Rock And Roll All Nite" in the intro.

■ She

Written by Gene Simmons and Stephen Coronel for the Wicked Lester album, "She" was remodelled on *Dressed To Kill* as a funky heavy rock track. Eight of the album's ten songs are knocked off inside three minutes, but "She" is stretched over four minutes as the band lock into a heavy, hypnotic groove.

■ Love Her All I Can

Another tune revived from the Wicked Lester sessions, "Love Her All I Can" is hardly one of Paul Stanley's best-known songs, but as on "Anything For My Baby", there's plenty of spirit and energy in the delivery.

Leigh Marklew: "*Dressed to Kill* is a great album and I managed a great, personal Kiss moment in honour of it. When we were in New York in 1993 recording the second Terrorvision album *How To Make Friends And Influence People*, our label put together a photo session that would be used on the inside sleeve of the record. And to my utter delight they let us choose Bob Gruen to capture four herberts from Bradford having the absolute time of their lives. Now, all those Kiss aficionados out there should recognize the name of Bob Gruen as a prominent photographer of Kiss in their earlier years. Indeed, he shot the famous 'Kiss in suits' sleeve for *Dressed To Kill*. So, when he had finished a few rolls of us posing away on our balcony at the Chelsea Hotel, I very politely asked him if he would walk for two minutes with us and recreate the *Dressed To Kill* shot on the VERY SAME STREET CORNER in Manhattan that he had done with Ace, Gene, Paul and Peter some 20 years earlier. He couldn't have been more obliging. He even dragged some anecdotes of the 1973 session out of his memory banks. Anyway, after trying to put the other boys into roughly the same poses as Kiss, I joined them on the end in Gene's place and sneered and leered into the Nikon. Pure rock 'n' roll bliss! 'Love Her All I Can' is great because it's the exact opposite of what the 'Crazy Nights'-era Kiss was all about."

■ Rock And Roll All Night

The daddy of all Kiss anthems. "You drive us wild, we'll drive you crazy," sings Gene Simmons on

Peter Criss: spot the dummy

this, confirming the special bond between Kiss and their rapidly-growing audience. An opening blast of six powerchords became the cue for dazzling on-stage pyrotechnics and the chorus, sung gang-style, was ready made for a sold-out concert arena. What kid in mid-70s America wasn't ready to rock and roll all night and party every day? If any one song defines Kiss, this most certainly is it.

Howard Johnson: "You can't dislike 'Rock And Roll All Nite', can you? It's neanderthal, it's gumby, it's dumb, it's inane, it's brilliant. If anybody doesn't like it, they must fuck off and buy something from the New Age section, because that's what it's all about, isn't it?"

Joe Mackett: "I remember walking out of Wembley Arena with loads of people piling into the tube station singing 'Rock And Roll All Nite'. It's just a classic."

Andy Hunns: "I love this but to me there's a bit of sadness attached to that song because it always signals the end of a Kiss show. As much as I love it, every time I see Kiss I know it's the last song as soon as that drumming starts."

Graham Stroud: "Certain songs are just classics: Cheap Trick's 'Surrender', Boston's 'More Than A Feeling', and 'Rock And Roll All Nite'. The studio version is actually a bit plodding, but when you see Kiss live and you're standing there with a big grin on your face and three inches of confetti on your head, it's brilliant. You've forgotten about your crappy job. It's the best comedy you'll ever see, although I wouldn't allow someone who isn't a Kiss fan to say that. I'd be challenging them: what band do you know that's sold three million lunch boxes?"

ALIVE!

The Album that transformed Kiss from cult heroes to all-American superstars, *Alive!* is now recognised as one of the great live rock recordings. By 1975 Kiss were headlining shows at major sports arenas. When the *Dressed To Kill* tour reached Detroit on

Skinny-legged Kiss celebrate the success of Alive!

March 27, 1975, the band hired famed producer Eddie Kramer to record the gig at the Motor City's prestigious 12,000-capacity Cobo Hall. Kramer was already a part of the Kiss story, having produced the five-song demo with which the group sealed their record contract with Casablanca.

After Detroit, Kramer recorded subsequent shows in Wildwood, New Jersey, Davenport, Iowa, and Cleveland, Ohio, although the bulk of *Alive!* is taken from the Cobo Hall concert. Kiss would later repay the loyalty of their Detroit fanbase with the anthem "Detroit Rock City".

Alive! features all the classic Kiss songs from the first three albums, kicking off with the frenetic "Deuce" and climaxing with "Rock And Roll All Nite" before the encore "Let Me Go, Rock'N'Roll". "Rock And Roll All Nite" was extracted as a single and rocketed to the upper reaches of the American chart – at last, the hit that label boss Neil Bogart had craved!

With a sell-out crowd roaring their approval, *Alive!* captured the energy of "The Hottest Band In The Land" (as Kiss were rather modestly billing themselves in 1975) better than the preceding studio albums. *Alive!* didn't tell the whole story – these were the days before simultaneous video and DVD releases – but fans could picture the scene as they turned up the volume on their record players and stared at the posters on their walls and the photos of fire-breathing and flashbombs on the album's gatefold sleeve.

What *Alive!* proved – emphatically – was that Kiss's music was strong enough to stand on its own. And Paul Stanley's between-song raps are especially entertaining: notably his introduction to "Cold Gin", where he declares: "I was talking to somebody backstage before, and they were telling me there's a lot of you people out there that like to drink vodka and orange juice!" Of course, as Stanley notes, "There's only one thing that's gonna do it the way you want it to," and that, as the audience yell at him, is "Cold Gin". Priceless stuff.

Alive! quickly reached gold status in the US for 500,000 sales, and has since gone on to sell more than four million copies in America alone.

Tracklisting: "Deuce", "Strutter", "Got To Choose", "Hotter Than Hell", "Firehouse", "Nothin' To Lose", "C'mon And Love Me", "Parasite", "She", "Watchin' You", "100,000 Years", "Black Diamond", "Rock Bottom", "Cold Gin", "Rock And Roll All Nite", "Let Me Go, Rock 'N'Roll".

DESTROYER

By 1976 Kiss were one of the biggest bands in America, but their hunger for success was unabated. With their fourth studio album, *Destroyer*, they adopted the motto passed on to Gene Simmons by his mother Flora: reach for the sky.

To create music on a grander scale to anything they had previously recorded, Kiss enlisted producer Bob Ezrin, whose impressive CV listed classic albums by Lou Reed and Alice Cooper. As the band set to work with Ezrin at New York's Record Plant studios, they received news that *Alive!* had achieved platinum status for one million sales. Inspired to raise the bar even higher, Kiss honed nine new songs to perfection, with Ezrin broadening the scope of the group's music by incorporating choirs, orchestration and an array of sound effects.

Def Leppard singer Joe Elliott: Destroyer is his favourite Kiss album

Released on March 15, 1976, and boasting cover art by illustrator Ken Kelly which portrayed the group as rock 'n' roll's ultimate superheroes, *Destroyer* was a stunning achievement which initially met with poor sales. Fans were shocked by Kiss's new polished sound, but once the band had returned to the road with their most extravagant stageshow to date, *Destroyer* quickly reached triple-platinum status. For many Kiss fanatics, among them Def Leppard singer Joe Elliott, *Destroyer* remains their greatest triumph.

■ Detroit Rock City

Rock fans in the Motor City had taken Kiss to their hearts before most of America had wised up, so as a thank-you to the audience immortalised on *Alive!*, Kiss delivered "Detroit Rock City", a blast of high-octane rock which soon replaced "Deuce" as the curtain-raiser for Kiss shows. Penned by Paul Stanley and Bob Ezrin, "Detroit Rock City" was made all the more dramatic by Ezrin's clever production. It begins with a radio news report of a fatal car crash as a Kiss fan revs up his car and goes for a spin to the sound of "Rock And Roll All Nite". At the song's climax is a screech of tyres and a shuddering head-on collision: a breathtaking piece of rock 'n' roll drama.

Joe Mackett: "Every rock fan who's heard that song wants it to be Manchester Rock City, Newcastle Rock City, Milan Rock City, or in my case, Llwyngwril Rock City! I've sung that a few times myself. Detroit is the Birmingham of America – car factories, heavy industry – not the kind of place that you'd choose to visit. But if there's one place that you'd want to see Kiss, it's Detroit, more so than New York. You get the feeling that Detroit is the rock capital of America. To put it into a British context, if I want to see a heavy metal festival in Britain, I go to Castle Donington."

Andy Hunns: "It's the opening track of a Kiss show. It's Gene and Ace walking down the ramps, it's Paul strutting his stuff. It's also synonymous with the funniest thing I've ever seen at a Kiss show. They opened with it at Stafford Bingley Hall in 1980 and Paul thought his guitar was out of tune. Gene took over lead vocal because Paul is swapping guitars. Stanley's going mental with his guitar tech. He's throwing guitars on and hitting it and it still sounds out of tune. And after three guitar changes he looks across and sees Ace leaning against the amps playing completely out of tune. But it didn't spoil the song."

Graham Stroud: "The studio version's great but I love the explosions on the *Alive II* version. I know exactly where every explosion comes in!"

Dave Reynolds: "Probably the greatest Kiss song of all time. No-one has been able to play this song as well as Kiss – and many have tried. With its atmospheric build-up, where you feel that you really are in the car with this drunk on his way to meet his maker while en route to, we presume, a Kiss gig, and the bombastic nature of the song, 'Detroit Rock City' is an absolute classic heavy metal song. And the addition of Eric Carr to the band in 1980 gave the track a further kick live, thanks to the Fox's use of double bass drums."

Mark Taylor: "Like so many other people, 'Detroit Rock City' is the song that pulled me into Kiss world."

■ King Of The Night Time World

As the clatter of crunching metal subsides at the sudden, shocking conclusion of "Detroit Rock City", Ace Frehley teases out the first spiralling notes of "King Of The Night Time World", keeping the adrenaline pumping. To maximise the dramatic effect, these two songs would be performed back-to-back for years to come.

Written by Stanley and Ezrin, with help from Mark Anthony and enigmatic rock svengali Kim Fowley, "King Of The Night Time World" is a tale of dangerous, high-rolling glamour set to thrilling, fast-paced hard rock riffing.

Andy Hunns: "I always relate 'King Of The Night Time World' to 'Detroit Rock City' finishing. When 'Detroit . . .' ends, I want that riff. I've seen them live when they haven't followed 'Detroit . . .' with 'King Of The Night Time World', and

Kim Fowley, co-author of "King Of The Night Time World"

gleeful wailing and giggling, which sounds positively demonic in context.

Joe Mackett: "When Kiss play 'God Of Thunder' live, with Gene high up above the stage looking demonic, you really can feel the earth move beneath you."

Dave Reynolds: "Despite the fact that Paul wrote it with every intention of using it as a vehicle for his own ego, fate decreed that this song belonged to Gene! Gene IS the God Of Thunder (And Rawk 'N' Rowl!). This track is about blood raining on the Kiss Army from the heavens. It's about a drum solo. It's about everything great at a Kiss show!"

Gary Banton: "This track really stands out with its dark production. A real epic! When I was 11 or 12 and I used to play this, I always used to turn my stereo down or cough loudly when Gene sang the 'rob you of your virgin soul' lyric! Ha ha! I used to think the word 'virgin' was rude! Well, I was young!"

■ Great Expectations

Gene Simmons likens the role of *Destroyer*'s producer Bob Ezrin to that of George Martin on the Beatles records, which turned the young Simmons on to rock'n'roll in the 1960s, and nowhere is Ezrin's influence more evident than on Simmons and Ezrin's "Great Expectations". Over a melodramatic orchestral theme, Simmons sings in the manner of an old show tune, although his subject matter is reassuringly familiar: at a Kiss show, an impressionable fan gazes in awe at her idol as Simmons flicks his tongue and teases: "You wish you were the one I was doing it to".

■ Flaming Youth

British rock heroes The Who were an early influence on the members of Kiss, and in "Flaming Youth", Kiss had their own youthful rallying cry in the vein of The Who's "My Generation". Written by Simmons, Stanley, Frehley and Ezrin, "Flaming Youth" blazes with positive energy and celebrates rock'n'roll as a life-affirming force, its chorus accompanied by a bizarre funfair carousel motif.

it's so disappointing if they don't. You want it! You're pushed to find two better opening tracks to an album."

■ God Of Thunder

As Gene Simmons's signature song – in which the giant bassist performs a bizarre onstage ritual, spitting out a mouthful of blood which dribbles off his inhumanly long tongue – "God Of Thunder" possesses mythical status among Kiss fans. Strange, then, that the song should be written not by Simmons but by Paul Stanley (a demo version of the song with vocals by Stanley can be found on the 2001 Kiss box set).

Stanley's skill is in making "God Of Thunder" the perfect vehicle for Simmons, who bellows "I command you to kneel!" with all the stagey, doom-mongering bravura of a comicbook super-hero. Adding to the surreal atmosphere is a child's

Dave Reynolds: "It's a close fight between 'Sweet Pain' and 'Flaming Youth', but the latter wins due to its anthemic nature.

"I always thought it was cool that the writer of the first Kiss Marvel Comic used the phrase 'Heads up Flaming Youth! Hither cometh thy destiny!' when throwing them the talisman box that turned Kiss into superheroes!"

■ Sweet Pain

With its kinky title and insistent riff, "Sweet Pain" is a stereotypical Gene Simmons rocker, although the use of female backing singers adds a fresh twist, especially when Simmons is joined in his sexual boast: "My love will drive you insane". However, the most remarkable feature of this song is the absence of guitarist Ace Frehley, who is replaced on lead by Dick Wagner.

Gary Banton: "A real hidden gem, this one. Great riffs, cool lyrics and of course those Gene moans. As we all now know, "Sweet Pain" features Dick Wagner playing the solo in an Ace-style.

Jeff Beck: not married to Peter Criss

Shame Ace couldn't miss that card game – I'd love to hear what he would have played!"

■ Shout It Out Loud

After "Detroit Rock City" and "Rock And Roll All Nite", "Shout It Out Loud" is Kiss's most potent anthem. Written by Simmons and Stanley, who trade verses throughout, "Shout It Out Loud" begins at a fever pitch and stays there for the best part of three minutes. It's all-American cornball rock the way only Kiss know how. All that's missing are the cheerleaders.

Joe Mackett: "It's more of an actual song than 'Rock And Roll All Nite'. It's got such a great vibe. You can't help singing along to it. If I saw Kiss and they didn't play 'Shout It Out Loud', I'd be gutted."

Andy Hunns: "Every song on *Destroyer* is fantastic, and "Shout It Out Loud" is just a great pop-rock song."

Graham Stroud: "How many times can you say the same thing about rocking and rolling and partying every night? Kiss taught me so many ways of saying the same thing!"

■ Beth

Peter Criss's "Beth" became a surprise hit when DJs began flipping the "Detroit Rock City" single to play this sweet, string-laden love song. Public response was massive. "Beth" has since become a benchmark for the rock ballad. Written by the drummer in dedication to his wife Lydia, the song was originally titled "Beck", which Gene Simmons baulked at because it might be misconstrued as a homage to English guitar hero Jeff Beck. Criss's sentiment, however, was clear: such was the scale of Kiss's success, he was spending more and more time away from his wife, whether on lengthy tours or in recording studios. Criss poured out his longing in a song which would become a centrepiece of the Kiss live show as the drummer stepped out from behind his kit to sit at the edge of the stage, crooning soppily while tossing red roses to the ladies in the first few rows of the stalls.

Dante Bonutto: "It's a fantastic song, well-

Peter Criss: "I know you love complaining, but Beth, what can I do?"

produced, and I assume it's autobiographical, although Simmons always claimed it was more Ezrin's creation that Criss's. Simmons had changed the track title from 'Beck' because it would have been embarrassing – to Jeff Beck, mainly. You can picture him sitting there waiting for Peter Criss to come home . . ."

Chris Dale: "I don't necessarily like the song too much, but this was the Kiss song that you could play to your granny and she'd like it, so your parents would put up with the satanic posters in your bedroom! 'Beth' was a good song to win the family over with. The original lyrics on Peter's demo of 'Beth' say 'I know you love complaining,' so it's not so much a love song as a stop-nagging-me song."

■ Do You Love Me?

"You love my seven-inch . . .leather heels," Paul Stanley teases before challenging his lover with "Do you love me?". On the evidence of this track, written by Stanley with Bob Ezrin and Kim Fowley, Kiss were feeling isolated by success and deeply suspicious of the women they were now encountering. The sneer in Stanley's vocal and the thumping that Peter Criss gives his kit make this one of the band's most convincing performances.

Howard Johnson: "It's a simple tune allied to a simple statement. 'You love my seven-inch leather heels . . .' – well, anyone who can write that has to be worthy of some consideration. The chimes are great at the end. And Paul Stanley was the first rapper – that bit where he says, 'I'm so tired of everybody saying it . . .if you really, really, really love me'. Forget your Grandmaster Flash, Paul Stanley invented rap music! He should be hailed and respected."

Graham Stroud: "You get a lot of bands writing songs about how depressed they're feeling, but not Kiss. 'Do You Love Me?' is all about concerts and studios and limousines and all the money, honey, that they're making. They're living this fantastic life and we all wish we could. Kiss have massive egos but I like to think it's done with tongue in cheek. If it's not, we're all in trouble."

Girl with future Def Leppard guitarist Phil Collen (second right)

Andy Hunns: "I saw Girl supporting Kiss and they did 'Do You Love Me?'. I thought, fair play to them. When you're a kid you love the support band, don't you? They're brilliant. Girl came on and I thought they were cool, and they had the bottle to do a Kiss song! You've got to give them credit, you know? All these plastic bottles and things were hurled at the stage."

Dante Bonutto: "Girl got thrown off the tour. I saw both nights at Wembley and they played 'Do You Love Me?' on the first night. Kiss had obviously told them not to play their song. Fair enough. But they played it and they didn't appear on the second night. I remember the announcer saying that Girl were not appearing that night, and a huge cheer went up."

Leigh Marklew: "Oops! I've said that Terrorvision never covered a Kiss song, but before we were Terrorvision, before we were the Spoilt Bratz and before Tony Wright was our singer, we used to knock out a very bad version of 'Do You Love Me?'. That was mainly down to our singer Julian's fixation with Paul Stanley. Mmm, very odd,

I know. I never heard if he grew a moustache and took to body building and great showtunes, but we did get ourselves a new singer! The track remains pure, pouting Paul at his seven-inch leather-heeled best!"

Dave Reynolds: "This is one of those great, cocky glam rock songs on which Paul reveals the kind of lifestyle that a rock star's groupie moll had become accustomed to. Bob Ezrin's production on this track really gives it a kinda Alice Cooper 'Elected' feel."

ROCK AND ROLL OVER

As its title implies, *Rock And Roll Over* saw Kiss going back to basics with a set of simple rock'n'roll songs. Despite its experimental nature, *Destroyer* had been a huge success, but Kiss decided on a return to the looser, grittier feel of their first three albums. With Eddie Kramer installed in the producer's chair once more, Kiss chose an unusual location for the recording of *Rock And Roll Over*. To capture the excitement and vibe of a Kiss concert, the band set up in the Nanuet Star Theater in New York State and played as if to a packed hall. The trick worked: *Rock And Roll Over* is one of Kiss's most vibrant records. The album was released on November 11, 1976, and was the first Kiss album to ship platinum with advance sales of one million copies.

■ I Want you

A surprising start: delicate acoustic guitar and singing from Paul Stanley before the whole band rocks out. Written by Stanley, "I Want You" is a vintage Kiss anthem that could have come from the very first album. It is also remarkable for Paul's stretching of the word "is". A sensational start to the album on which Kiss reaffirm their no-frills rock 'n' roll ethos. After the tricksy *Destroyer*, this was

business as usual for the biggest rock band in the United States.

Andy Hunns: "Brilliant opening, very quiet, and then Paul's screaming vocal: 'I WANT YOU!'."

■ Take Me

"Put your hand in my pocket, grab on to my rocket!" With an opening line like that, how could "Take Me" be anything but a Kiss classic? Stanley wrote the song with Sean Delaney as a celebration of the joys of oral sex, although on this evidence Stanley is less a giver than a taker, delighting in an image of his lover's head bobbing up and down in the moonlight.

Dave Reynolds: "It was often the second song in the set list on the *Love Gun* tour and is a classic example of Kiss at their best. And the lyrics are ridiculously superb."

A sulking Paul wishes he had Ace's epaulettes

Calling Dr. Love

The first of a double-whammy of Gene Simmons signature songs, "Calling Dr. Love" casts Simmons as the cure-all to any sexual hangups. Famous for the way it was introduced by Paul Stanley on *Alive II* as a song for anyone who's got "rock'n'roll pneumonia", the song's tongue-in-cheek lyrics are delivered over an exaggeratedly slow riff which is helped along by some clonking cowbell from Peter Criss.

Andy Hunns: "My favourite Gene Simmons song. It's one of his funniest. I love it when Gene goes, 'Oh yeah!'. A lot of people think of 'God Of Thunder' as Gene's song, but for me, 'Calling Dr. Love' is."

Joe Mackett: "I'm 16, wearing flares, a heavy metal T-shirt or a lumberjack shirt – long before the lumberjack shirt regained its credibility with grunge – and a leather jacket with tassels along the sleeves and cut-off denim jacket over the top. I'm looking very geeky with my pseudo-long hair, which is struggling to get past the collar. I'm standing in the youth club and I think I'm the cool one because I've been to America. And I am Dr. Love!"

Ladies Room

And where better for Dr. Love to set up his practice than in the ladies room? "For my money," Gene Simmons winks to us, "you can't be too soon." "Ladies Room" is livelier than "Calling Dr. Love", with Simmons' bass upfront on a bouncy riff and more rattling of the cowbell from Criss. So there will be no prizes for guessing what the Catman got for Christmas.

Tony Cooke: "I used to wear make-up when I was going to rock clubs. Not like Kiss, just a cheeky bit of eyeliner, that was all, no lipstick, the hair all glammed up. And you'd always go into the ladies room to do it. If the bouncers had a problem with that, you'd go, 'It's cool, man. Kiss! "Ladies Room"!' I've been in ladies toilets since, but that's a bit too rock'n'roll to get into here. Lots of things happen in the ladies room, don't they? It's a lot more sexy than the gents."

Baby Driver

This swaggering, old-fashioned rock 'n' roller is the work of Peter Criss and Stan Penridge. Criss belts out the dumbass lyrics over one of the album's coolest riffs.

Love 'Em And Leave 'Em

If ever a title of a Kiss song summed up its author's commitment to relationships, it is Gene Simmons' "Love 'Em And Leave 'Em". In the first line of the song, Simmons is approached by a girl who asks which hotel he's staying at. In the blink of an eye she's hiking up her dress and Simmons is having his way. By the time he's sung the chorus, the girl is forgotten. Simmons recites this familiar story over a Motown-inspired backbeat.

Mr. Speed

Overlooked by all but the most fanatical Kiss fans, "Mr. Speed" is a great little rocker buzzing with spontaneity and seemingly cooked up in a matter of minutes. Written by Paul Stanley and Sean Delaney, "Mr. Speed" is a routine tale of Stanley's sexual prowess freshened by an infectious melody, hooky riff and loose, off-the-cuff performance.

See You In Your Dreams

A brisk pop-rock number reprised two years later on Simmons' solo album, "See You In Your Dreams" is his ultimate ego trip. After consoling a lonely partygoer, Simmons does not shag her – a first for a Kiss song – but promises that she'll see him and feel him in her dreams that night. Where does Gene Simmons get off? On himself, clearly.

Hard Luck Woman

Written by Paul Stanley and sung by Peter Criss, this pretty tune was *Rock And Roll Over*'s big hit single, peaking at number 11 on the US chart. In spite of (or, perhaps, because of) a somewhat comical reference to a "sailor's only daughter" and

Gene Simmons: now that's an axe!

"child of the water", "Hard Luck Woman" is one of Kiss's most charming songs, evocative of Rod Stewart's classic mid-70s singles. The wider public took to "Hard Luck Woman" as they had to Criss's "Beth". Its success owes all to Paul Stanley, who not only wrote the song but was smart enough to encourage Criss to sing it. As with "God Of Thunder", "Hard Luck Woman" would become a signature for its singer rather than its composer.

Dante Bonutto: "I had visions of her living on a beach in an upturned boat, collecting sea shells . . ."

■ Makin' Love

On an album filled with breezy, feelgood rock, the heavy metal crunch of "Makin' Love" comes as a surprise finish. Written by Paul Stanley and Sean Delaney, this is the heaviest song the band recorded in the 1970s. The riff was copied by countless rock bands through the 70s and 80s.

Andy Hunns: "How many times has that riff been ripped? It's not a millions miles from Riot's 'Swords And Tequila', which was not a million miles from Iron Maiden's '2 Minutes To Midnight'. It's Zeppelin's 'Communication Breakdown', but it's Kiss's version. It's Kiss's metal song. Kiss aren't a metal band, they're just a great pop rock 'n' roll band, but 'Makin' Love' is their metal song."

LOVE GUN

By the summer of 1977 Kiss were officially declared the most popular band in the US in a poll of the nation's school kids and teenagers conducted by Gallup. This was confirmed on June 30 when Kiss's sixth studio recording, *Love Gun*, was certified platinum upon its release with pre-order sales of one million units. On the same day, Marvel Comics launched the first Kiss comicbook amid controversy: the band had mixed their own blood into the ink shortly before the issue went to press!

Like its predecessor *Rock And Roll Over*, the Eddie Kramer-produced *Love Gun* was ahard-edged rock record on which guitarist Ace Frehley finally made his vocal debut singing lead on his own composition, "Shock Me". This was the first time that all four band members had sung lead on the same album.

Again, Ken Kelly created a powerful image for the album's cover, picturing Kiss standing in an exotic temple with a harem of face-painted women at their feet. Inevitably, Kiss hit the road with their most expensive stage production to date shortly after *Love Gun*'s release.

■ I Stole Your Love

Continuing the back-to-basics approach of *Rock And Roll Over*, *Love Gun* begins at breakneck pace with the hard and fast rock'n'roll of Paul Stanley's "I Stole Your Love". Stanley is in outrageously cocky mood, gloating at a hard-hearted lover and screaming "Guitar!" to cue a cool, off-the-cuff solo from Ace Frehley.

Dave Reynolds: "Although it sounds a bit too lightweight in its studio form on *Love Gun*, "I Stole Your Love" took on an altogether different shape live. In actual fact, Kiss opened up with this song on the *Love Gun* tour. An up-and-at-'em rocker that, if you listen carefully, can be traced to having roots in the way Deep Purple constructed 'Burn'. I like the way Paul describes how he turned this chick he was dating who was being a little stand-offish with him into someone who suddenly realised she needed him a whole lot more than she first thought. 'How does it feel, to find out you're failin' your test?'"

Dante Bonutto: "Some of my favourite Kiss tracks were the ones that worked well live, and I think they used to start the show with 'I Stole Your Love'."

■ Christine Sixteen

Of the many sleazy songs that Gene Simmons has written during thirty years as Kiss's resident dirtbag, none is sleazier than "Christine Sixteen", in which Simmons propositions a schoolgirl and sighs, "I've got to have her". Over plonking boogie-woogie piano, Simmons recalls his first sighting of Christine in a voice as proper as his intentions are clearly not.

Joe Mackett: "I was 16 when I first heard it, and I remember thinking: Why can't I meet girls like that?"

Leigh Marklew: "Ever the romantic, I prefer Gene's ode to an underage cutie rather than to a fried old groupie who makes plaster casts of rock stars' dicks. I love the honky tonk piano on this and the off-beat rhythms are totally fresh as well. Do you think the spoken piece in the middle would work in a Yorkshire accent?"

■ Got Love For Sale

Another hard-rocking Simmons tune wherein the growling bassist offers himself to any woman who'll have him. If the theme is familiar, a funky refrain lifts the song out of the ordinary, as does some tricky string-bending from Ace Frehley.

■ Shock Me

It took six albums, but Ace Frehley finally delivers his first lead vocal on "Shock Me". Like his hero Rolling Stone Keith Richards, Ace hasn't got the greatest voice but it's a great rock'n'roll voice, and his shaky, half-cut style brings a certain wasted cool to the song's sado-masochistic fantasies and cheeky electrical puns.

Leigh Marklew: "I've always loved Ace and I think his first appearance on record as a singer is still his best. This track also has some exemplary rhyming of 'leather', 'better' and 'altogether', all delivered in a brilliant New Yawk drawl. There have been times, I'm sure, when all of us have been DOWN TO THE BARE WIRE! Great drumming and top guitar solo. Perfick!"

■ Tomorrow And Tonight

A typically exuberant Paul Stanley party number, "Tomorrow And Tonight" picks up where "Rock And Roll All Nite" left off. A clever detail has female backing singers taking up the chorus during a Rolling Stones-inspired breakdown after Stanley has, amusingly, rhymed "cellar" with "fella".

Graham Stroud: "'We can rock all day, we can roll all night.' Nuff said! It's the way you'd love to

be able to live your life. However much we're into it, we can never rock all day and roll all night, but we always sing it. It's escapism. Entertainment and escapism: that's Kiss."

■ Love Gun

If one Kiss song embodies the full-on rock'n'roll persona of Paul Stanley, it is "Love Gun". Over that famous staccato machine-gun riff, Stanley is at his horniest as he delivers one of the all-time classic Kiss lyrics: "No place for hiding, baby, no place to run, you pulled the trigger of my…love gun!"

Howard Johnson: "That lyric seems silly now, but at the time I thought, 'Man, it's genius!' It's clever – trigger, gun. Clever enough for me, anyway. I also like the military-style drum tattoo."

Joe Mackett: "I love Paul hamming it up on stage. 'What's that in your pocket?'. 'Baby, that's my love gun!'."

Andy Hunns: "Spinal Tap must have listened to those lyrics. And they must have been writing it thinking, how do we get the noise of a gun? Da-da-da-da, da-da-da-da! It's just a fantastic pop song. And it's a song about a knob!"

Graham Stroud: "When I was in Japan, I went to a football match. Japanese football is very odd. We were watching the choreographed crowd chanting. They have this guy with a drum and the crowd all clap along. It was halfway through the second half and the guy struck up the beat from 'Love Gun'. I couldn't believe it, I was gobsmacked. I said to the girl sitting next to me, who didn't speak much English, 'Love Gun. Kiss,' and she said, 'Yes'. It was a bizarre moment."

Gary Banton: "You've gotta admire Paul Stanley for writing this song as completely as he did. Anyone who has heard his demo of this track knows that the final version is almost identical. Paul had already written the parts for all the instruments and played them himself on the demo. Indeed, he plays the bass on the final recorded version. And who else, apart from maybe Gene or David Lee Roth, could have written an anthemic ode to their penis?"

■ Hooligan

Having revealed his soft, sentimental side with the previous year's hit ballad "Beth", Peter Criss reaffirms his bad boy credentials with the self-explanatory "Hooligan". The riff is pure attitude and Criss bristles with Italian-American New York bravado as he sneers comically: "I'm a hooligan, won't go to school again."

Dante Bonutto: "The worst song that Kiss ever recorded, I think."

■ Almost Human

Gene Simmons recreates the menace of Hotter Than Hell's "Watchin' You" on "Almost Human", one of the most bizarre songs in the Kiss catalogue. An underplayed, off-kilter chorus adds to the track's surreal atmosphere as a "hungry" Simmons begs for understanding and creature comfort.

Leigh Marklew: "This is like an update on 'Watchin' You'. Another grinding, guttural Simmons stomper. And, mmm, yes – I'm getting a few oriental notes on the back of the palate along with a hint of early funk as an aftertaste. Splendid!"

Chris Dale: "I'm one of those fans that Gene Simmons hates, the kind who always whinge about setlists, who want to see Eric Singer in hawk make-up, who want a Wicked Lester reunion tour, who love it when Ace trips up onstage, and always want Kiss to play obscure songs like 'Almost Human'."

■ Plaster Caster

Gene Simmons named this song in tribute to the most notorious and dedicated groupies in America, who made casts of the erect members of their favourite rock bands. A loose, garage-rock feel adds to the delightful tackiness of Simmons's lyrics.

Andy Hunns: "It's the closest that Kiss ever came to a garage-rock song, really rough, raw early 70s stuff. It was like Kiss's version of a New York punk song."

■ Then She Kissed Me

In covering this pop classic – a hit for The Crystals in 1963 – Kiss change the sex of the song's key players but stick to the original arrangement and melody as faithfully as is possible for a four-piece hard rock band. Paul Stanley sings lead with a genuine affection for the Phil Spector era and Ace contributes a lovely, restrained solo. A strange end to the album, but as they proved with the first album's "Kissin' Time", Kiss were masters of sly brand extension.

The Crystals, whose 1963 pop classic got a kitsch Kiss makeover

Howard Johnson: "Kiss were kitsch rock. I never believed in them when they were trying to be mean on 'War Machine'. It seemed fake when they were hard rockin' muthas. I liked them when they were very poppy, a bit bubblegum, cartoonish and wilfully dumb. 'Then She Kissed Me' was brilliant and totally kitsch. And very faithful apart from the title, although it would have worked equally well either way. I like pop rock, genuine pop songs played with a bit of pizazz."

ALIVE II

"You wanted the best and you got the best! The hottest band in the world: Kiss!" With this hysterical announcement, Kiss set about topping their break-through album *Alive!* with another heavyweight in-concert recording.

Trusted producer Eddie Kramer was again at the helm as with *Alive!*. Kramer recorded four shows at the Los Angeles Forum when Kiss's *Love Gun* tour reached the West Coast in August 1977. For many fans, these performances were even more exciting than those captured on *Alive!*. Kicking off with the definitive version of "Detroit Rock City", *Alive II* featured the best of the three post-*Alive!* studio albums: *Destroyer*, *Rock And Roll Over* and *Love Gun*. The original vinyl release was a double album in a gatefold sleeve, which opened to reveal an amazing photo of Kiss's biggest stageshow to date: the band are poised on massive platforms ten feet above the stage amid columns of fire and shooting sparks. The fourth side of vinyl featured the added bonus of five new studio tracks recorded at the Capitol Theatre in Passaic, New Jersey. Unknown to Kiss fans, Ace Frehley was absent from these sessions. Kiss enlisted their friend Bob Kulick to play guitar on four of the songs – Kulick had auditioned for Kiss back in 1973.

Tracklisting: "Detroit Rock City", "King Of The Night Time World", "Ladies Room", "Makin' Love", "Love Gun", "Calling Dr. Love", "Christine Sixteen", "Shock Me", "Hard Luck Woman", "Tomorrow And Tonight", "I Stole Your Love",

"Beth", "God Of Thunder", "I Want You", "Shout It Out Loud". Plus these new recordings:

■ All American Man

Paul Stanley sings this thumping hard rock tune with the kind of self-aggrandisement that was Kiss's trademark, dubbing himself "a six-foot, hot look, all-American man" and firing off a warning to any rival males who can't keep their women satisfied.

Howard Johnson: "I find it hilarious but I suspect he wrote it without his tongue in his cheek. He thought it was a clarion call to oral sex; I think it's a funny little tune."

Dave Reynolds: "For me, four of the five tracks on the fourth side of *Alive II* find Kiss at their peak. This is Kiss at their enormodome-packing, fire-breathing, blood-spitting, platform-booted best. Ironic, then, that Frehley barely contributed to the recording of these new studio tracks. As a track that's less than subtly aimed at groupies, "All American Man" doubtless encouraged a million wannabe rock stars to wave the stars and stripes and head for the ladies room – and have a million teenage girls wanting to meet them there. Sadly, to my knowledge, the only track from the five new songs recorded for *Alive II* that was ever played live was "Rocket Ride" – and that was only played by Ace in his Frehley's Comet days."

■ Rockin' In The USA

Continuing the all-American theme is Gene Simmons' "Rockin' In The USA", a playful number in which Simmons reels off his daftest lyric in corny homage to Kiss's homeland. France was okay, he notes, and in England there wasn't much to do, but his message is as unequivocal as it is cheesy: Kiss are happiest when they're rockin' in the USA!

■ Larger Than Life

Gene Simmons has never run out of ways to express his worth to womankind. Here he boasts "my love is larger than life". Simmons' bluster is backed up by a powerhouse performance by drummer Peter Criss.

Dave Reynolds: "While 'All American Man' is

Kiss: larger than life

very much the Paul Stanley showcase on the fourth side of *Alive II*, 'Larger Than Life' is all Gene. Huge drums, skyscraper riffs and some wicked lead guitar work, this captured the predatory side of Simmons' nature – y'know, the one that's constantly chasing skirt – perfectly."

■ Rocket Ride

If Ace Frehley let the side down by failing to show for these sessions, he did his best to compensate with "Rocket Ride", the strongest of *Alive II*'s five studio tracks. Frehley not only wrote the song in conjunction with Sean Delaney, he also sings lead vocal and plays guitar and bass. The lyric is typical of the "Space Ace" who complained of the weight of gravity on Earth in *Alive!*'s liner notes. Moreover, his brilliant lead work proved that despite Bob Kulick's flair and dependability, Ace Frehley was still indispensable to Kiss.

Dante Bonutto: "I liked the idea of having these extra studio tracks on a live album, and 'Rocket Ride' is a classic Ace Frehley track. He's definitely on this one – isn't he?"

■ Any Way You Want It

Kiss paid their respects to their early influences with this cover of a Dave Clark Five hit from the 1960s, an upbeat British pop nugget which clearly had an effect on Kiss's own populist approach. If this track was recorded under strain following Ace Frehley's no-show, there is no hint of tension in this breezy performance.

The Dave Clark Five: the man on the left has just heard Kiss' version of "Any Way You Want It"

THE SOLO ALBUMS

In 1978, Kiss's superstardom was confirmed beyond all doubt with the simultaneous release of four solo albums. 1.25 million copies of each album were shipped to record stores throughout the United States in anticipation of huge public demand, and although sales would eventually prove a little disappointing, the solo albums proved a creative triumph, allowing each band member to explore new styles of music and express their individuality. The portrait cover art for the albums was shrewdly themed to enhance their collectability.

ACE FREHLEY

The most successful of the Kiss solo albums was that of guitarist Ace Frehley, due to the hit single "New York Groove". Frehley recorded the album's nine tracks in a home studio built to his exact specifications in the basement of his Connecticut mansion. He hired Eddie Kramer to produce the record after Kramer's solid work on several Kiss albums. The result was the toughest-sounding of the solo albums, an unabashed heavy rock record on which Frehley proved himself a more than capable singer and frontman. This new confidence was surely a major factor in Frehley's decision to quit the group for a solo career some years later.

■ Rip It Out

Just as "Strutter" had made a huge impact as the opening song on Kiss's debut, so "Rip It Out" began Ace's album in emphatic style, a blast of high-powered hard rock in which drummer Anton Fig performs with a raw power that must have put the fear of God into Peter Criss. Fig would later record with Kiss when Criss lost interest in the group. Of course, Ace is the star of the show, and on "Rip It Out" his guitar playing is electrifying. What's more, his raw, sneering vocal has such an authority that Kiss fans must have wondered why it took the guitarist all of six albums to muster the confidence to sing lead.

■ Speedin' Back To My Baby

Co-written with wife Jeanette, "Speedin' Back To My Baby" keeps the energy level high with a barrelling rock 'n' roll riff and a pretend-dumb lyric in which Ace exclaims: "Speedin' back to my baby!

Ace Frehley: kiss me quick!

And I don't mean maybe!" Ace would explore the darker reaches of his music on this album, but on this track he's simply letting his hair down and having fun.

Howard Johnson: "It's one of my favourites – and I don't mean maybe. In my view, 'Speedin' Back To My Baby', coming from Ace Frehley, has got nothing to do with driving a car. For that very reason it's great. Ace's is my favourite solo album. He can't sing but there's something appealing about his voice."

Leigh Marklew: "Honorable mention goes to 'Speeding Back To My Baby' because it inspired Terrorvision's motto for our Total Vegas label. Sin querer decir quizas – not meaning maybe!"

■ Snowblind

Although not a cover of Black Sabbath's infamous cocaine anthem, "Snow Blind" nevertheless hinted at the drug-assisted mania which so many of Ace Frehley's rock star peers succumbed to in the decadent 70s. Over a twisting riff, Frehley spills out a lyric full of confusion and doubt. "I'm lost in space," Ace groans. For once, his spaced-out alien schtick had a ring of desperation.

■ Ozone

One of the most inventive songs on the album, the complex riffs and whacked-out melody of "Ozone" are the sound of Ace Frehley reaching deeper than he had ever done within the confines of Kiss to create the most original and personal music of his career. "I'm the kind of guy who likes getting high," Ace reveals with an echo of the preceding "Snow Blind", but clever use of acoustic and electric guitars and exotic percussion makes "Ozone" anything but a regulation dope song.

■ What's On Your Mind?

For all the hard rock dynamics on Ace's album, there is also a well-defined pop sensibility to songs like "What's On Your Mind?", blending punchy riffing with a softly descending chorus melody. Ace always looked at things a little differently, and here his unorthodox thinking pays off.

■ New York Groove

Originally recorded by Hello in the 1970s, "New York Groove" was written by Russ Ballard, who would later provide hit material for Ritchie Blackmore's Rainbow with "Since You Been Gone" and "I Surrender". With its funky shuffle and cod-soul hookline, "New York Groove" gave Frehley the hit single that eluded Stanley, Simmons and Criss.

Russ Ballard, New York groover

■ I'm In Need Of Love

With a riff that lurches like a drunk and lyrics in which Frehley begs for affection, "I'm In Need Of Love" is the closest that Ace Frehley has come to penning a bar-room blues. Unexpectedly, Ace shakes off his apparent lethargy to lead a frenzied midsection with rapid-fire soloing.

Leigh Marklew: "I think I'm correct in believing this was the best selling of the solo albums, which probably led, ultimately, to Ace's demise within the band. The inflation of his ego and the battering taken by Gene's and Paul's albums put the writing on the wall. Top fucking album though. I love the OTT drum/guitar solo in the middle of 'Rip It Out', but 'I'm In Need Of Love' is even better, being totally spaced-out and shambolic."

■ Wiped-Out

"I was as blind as a skunk!" Frehley hollers on "Wiped-Out", his equivalent of an Alcoholics Anonymous confessional. If the lyric is a shameless admission of booze-fuelled madness, the music is a mishmash of fast and slow riffing and cartoonish vocals. Here, more than at any other time in his career, Ace Frehley truly sounds like a man on the edge – or a drunken fool having the time of his life.

■ Fractured Mirror

To end the album, Ace plays a brilliant instrumental. "Fractured Mirror" is at once heavy and beautifully melodic, a spell-binding finish to an album which delighted fans, surprised critics and set off a little voice in Ace Frehley's head that said, "I can do it without these guys…".

Howard Johnson: "It's a drug album, let's be honest. And I really like some of the weird guitar sounds when it breaks out in that mad solo. He's an appaling guitar player, but he's got a certain style about him, and I don't think Kiss is about how well you can play."

Rudy Reed: "The greatest track Kiss never wrote. 'Fractured Mirror' had the same effect on me as Led Zeppelin's 'Kashmir'. When I first got the album I had to listen to it twelve times back-to-back, I loved it so much. Somebody really should do a contemporary remix of this song. When I bought the four solo albums I made my own compilation of the best songs from the albums, and I even imagined a concert where they'd play just solo material. 'Fractured Mirror' was always the first encore."

PAUL STANLEY

Ace Frehley's album sold more, but it was Paul Stanley's that pointed to Kiss's immediate future

Paul Stanley, solo star

with a pop-rock feel that would be echoed in 1979's *Dynasty* and 1980's *Unmasked*. Stanley recorded his album in New York and Los Angeles with a group of experienced session musicians and close friends Bob Kulick and Carmine Appice. Kulick had recently stepped into Ace Frehley's shoes to play lead guitar on four of the studio tracks featured on *Alive II*. Appice was a well-known drummer whose CV lists spells in Vanilla Fudge and with Rod Stewart. Stanley's album is rich in variety, ranging from hard rock to pop and soul, but as a whole it is closer in spirit to Kiss than the other three solo albums, and certainly the most cohesive.

The Kulick brothers: Bruce (left) and Bob

■ Tonight You Belong To Me

With a title that's pure Paul Stanley, this is a sensational opening track, reminiscent of the classic "Black Diamond" with Stanley singing breathily over an acoustic guitar before switching to full-blown hard rock anthem mode. "Tonight You Belong To Me" expresses Paul Stanley's passion for music as powerfully as "Love Gun" or "Strutter" but with one minor difference: where Kiss songs exude macho arrogance, Stanley's solo songs tend toward the romantic. For all its hard rock pomp, "Tonight You Belong To Me" is not so much a boast as a plea.

Howard Johnson: "I think Bob Kulick's on this, and I really like him. I got to know him when he

was playing with Meat Loaf. What a nice bloke, what tremendously strong dope, and what a good guitar player. When I first went to New York I visited him at his apartment and he couldn't have been nicer. He had dope that could stun a rhino, and I wasn't experienced in these things. I ended up monged out listening to him playing guitar."

Graham Stroud: "I never thought I'd say this about a Kiss song, but it's beautiful. Really nice acoustic guitar and Paul sings it like he really means it. It's a real change for him, a risk, because it's not up-and-at-'em like Kiss. This is Paul's other side. It shows that he's not always a rocker. It's a sloppy song. How many more songs does he have to write about girls and partying? He's got balls for doing this song. It's totally different from anything Kiss have ever done. Paul is a visionary poet!"

Dante Bonutto: "Paul's album is an absolute classic and if you're a Kiss fan it's one of the best Kiss albums. The intro on 'Tonight You Belong To Me' is brilliant. You know it's going somewhere and it goes exactly where you want it to go. It's a real Paul Stanley track: he sings falsetto; he's pompous and preening. You can imagine him with the Ibanez guitar."

■ Move On

One of three songs co-written by Mikel Japp, "Move On" has Stanley reminiscing about the times he sat on his mother's knee as she dispensed advice to her boy on the complex issue of relationships. In the event of woman trouble, Paul refers to mom's simple maxim: "Move On". He delivers this tongue-in-cheek lyric in a sprightly pop-rock tune featuring some rather foxy-sounding female backup singers.

Graham Stroud: "Paul Stanley's solo album is the best Kiss album ever. It's a bit sad because he's the only member of Kiss on it, but it's pure pop. 'Move On' has got some great lyrics: 'A lot of pretty women gonna try and tie you down. 'I'm sure they will, Paul. Kiss is all about Paul Stanley to me, but if I went to see them and Gene didn't spit blood I'd be disappointed, and if Ace didn't try to shoot a rocket out of his guitar – unsuccessfully. If Peter didn't do a drum solo I'd be delighted."

■ Ain't Quite Right

Dropping the tempo significantly, Paul Stanley mixes smooth soul moves and some crisp power-chords on this slow-burner of a number. Such sophistication marked a major departure from the bombastic style of Kiss, as did Stanley's troubled, restless lyric.

■ Wouldn't You Like To Know Me

If the preceding "Ain't Quite Right" carries a hint of emotional vulnerability behind the mask of Paul Stanley, "Wouldn't You Like To Know Me?" is the back to the Stanley of "I Stole Your Love", very much in love with himself as he struts his stuff on this ballsy power-pop tune. This really is vintage Paul Stanley.

Rudy: "It's Paul Stanley's homage to himself. It's got more strut than 'Strutter'! It's one of the great songs to one's own self. Paul is just basking in his own brilliance."

Gary Banton: "It's an all-out rocker. Paul Stanley's solo album is pretty much the perfect rock album in my opinion (though Journey's *Escape* would give it a good run for its money!). Every song is a complete masterpiece and the musicianship is second to none."

■ Take Me Away (Together As One)

As its title suggests, this is a starry-eyed love song given a dreamlike quality by its gentle verses and Stanley's whispered, love-struck lyrics. Of course, being Paul Stanley from Kiss, he can't resist rocking out on the chorus, but this remains one of his most sensitive songs.

Gary Banton: "The emotion, the music, the lyrics, the vocals: it's all absolutely impeccable, and it still manages to send shivers down my spine every time I hear it."

Rudy Reed: "If I was Kiss's manager, I would have made Paul Stanley write seventy per cent of every Kiss album. Without a shadow of a doubt, he is the best songwriter in the band and this is a great moment."

Paul Stanley: wouldn't you like to know him?

■ It's Alright

For sheer energy and air-punching excitement, "It's Alright" is on a par with "Wouldn't You Like To Know Me?". In fact, it's right up there with "Love Gun". "It's alright if you want me," Stanley sings with the nonchalance that comes from being a world famous rock'n'roll superstar.

Leigh Marklew: "First there's 'Ain't Quite Right', then 'It's Alright'. Make your mind up, Paul – is it or isn't it? They're two of the top tracks from probably the most consistent solo album. The whole album is just pure, unadulterated, brilliant late 70s American pop rock. Like a cross between Kiss, Tom Petty, The Cars and Journey. The singing and playing match the songwriting on every track. Top notch!"

■ Hold Me, Touch Me (Think Of Me When We're Apart)

With its convoluted title and intimate lyrics, this is almost a companion piece to "Take Me Away (Together As One)", except that "Hold Me, Touch Me . . ." is even slushier, with Paul cooing over piano and softly-played strings. An angelic choir adds to the sense of camp, but this is a sincere song, and perhaps the bravest and most honest performance of Paul Stanley's career.

Tony Cooke: "This was the single and I like it because he was so cool. I felt I was Paul Stanley for about eight years of my life, although I didn't look anything like the bloke. I thought I was a cross between Paul Stanley and Ozzy's bass player, Rudy Sarzo. I didn't have the hairy chest, though. I was a glam rocker, a bit girly. I crimped my hair, lots of earrings. Hold Me, Touch Me . . was nice pop song."

■ Love In Chains

The sensitive soul of "Hold Me, Touch Me . . ." turns strutting Starchild once more on "Love In Chains", a melodramatic and near-hysterical rocker with a punchy chorus and plenty of flashy lead guitar. Lyrically, it's a first for Paul Stanley; "Love In Chains" is not the S&M anthem that might be expected, but a metaphor for Paul's sexual frustration.

■ Goodbye

Like Val Doonican, Paul Stanley rocks – but gently – on a bittersweet closing track that echoes the sentiment of Peter Criss's "Beth". 'I'm coming back, I swear it, somehow," Stanley declares over insistent riffing. Like Ace's "Fractured Mirror", "Goodbye" ends Paul's album on a melancholic note. Ostensibly a dedication to an estranged partner, "Goodbye" can also be interpreted as a message to Kiss fans. As Arnold Schwarzenegger put it: "I'll be back."

Rudy Reed: "Prince springs to mind here. I can imagine him covering this song. The lyrics are deep and poetic and soulful, the music is stunning and it's a great way to end the album."

GENE SIMMONS

Beginning with a suitably demonic cackle and ending with a bizarre take on the Disney theme "When You Wish Upon A Star", Gene Simmons's solo album is the most varied, surprising and adventurous of the four. Simmons relished the opportunity to record songs which he had written over a number of years and were considered too left-field for the Kiss repetoire.

He relocated to England to work on the album with producer Sean Delaney, recording in a studio housed in a barn near the historic university town of Oxford. The album is a star-studded affair. Simmons invited various celebrity friends to record with him, including Michigan rocker Bob Seger, MOR singer Helen Reddy, Aerosmith guitarist Joe Perry, singer-songwriter Janis Ian, disco diva Donna Summer and one-time paramour Cher. The result is an astonishing record which revealed many new sides to the fire-breathing God Of Thunder.

■ Radioactive

A mock-operatic intro mixing some dramatic orchestration with spooky choral "hosannas" recalls the other-worldly atmosphere of Simmons' signature "God Of Thunder", but "Radioactive" confounds expectations with a knockabout pop-

was the single, but there are so many other cool songs on that record."

■ Burning Up With Fever

Another bizarre opening as Simmons counts in a 1-2-3-4 by yelling off-mike before John Shane Howell plays classical guitar for a couple of bars – so clumsily and tunelessly that it has to be a joke. The song itself is a catchy funk-rock tune reminiscent of early Doobie Brothers, whose guitarist Jeff "Skunk" Baxter plays the strutting riff and a solo that's pure Ace Frehley. The soul-styled chorus recalls the Rolling Stones's "Tumbling Dice" and Kiss's Casablanca labelmate Donna Summer adds some brilliant ad-libs in the fadeout.

Leigh Marklew: "Gene's sense of Beatles-esque melody gets shoved to the front on his solo album and it's all the better for it. I could choose loads of tracks from this record, but I'll go with 'Burning Up With Fever' for the totally brilliant classical guitar intro!"

Gary Banton: "I love the diversity of styles Gene brings to his solo album, but this track stands out for me for a variety of reasons. The groove is happening, one of my faves, Jeff 'Skunk' Baxter (of Steely Dan and Doobie Brothers fame), plays some mad guitar and the gospel backing vocals rock the joint! The best part for me though is the last thirty or so seconds. As the song fades, gradually turn up your volume and check out Neil Jason's crazy and funky bass lines. They get me every time!"

Rudy Reed: "It gives you an insight into the man, with that shout and twisted little intro and then he stomps around. And clearly he must be talking about sex again! His music benefited from dating Cher and Diana Ross at this point."

■ See You Tonite

Gene Simmons makes no secret of his love of The Beatles and "See You Tonite" is his simple homage to the world's favourite pop group. A pretty acoustic tune in the same vein as Kiss's "Hard Luck Woman", it's one of the very best songs Simmons has ever written. Jeff "Skunk" Baxter features again.

Donna Summer, disco diva and friend of Gene Simmons

rock arrangement far removed from the cartoon rock stomp of "God Of Thunder". Written by Simmons alone, as were all but two of the album's eleven tracks, "Radioactive" was selected as the album's lead single. It features Bob Seger on back-up vocals and Joe Perry on guitar.

Dave Reynolds: "While Paul and Ace basically put together songs that could have made any Kiss album, and Peter cut a record that was pretty well dismissed by all and sundry (but rather underrated, I feel), Gene's record was a revelation and a template as to how a solo album should be recorded. Invite loads of your mates down and have fun. He had some great stuff on there and a lot of great people contributing to it. I pick 'Radioactive' because it

■ Tunnel Of Love

In the context of a Kiss album, "Tunnel Of Love" might have been a heavy-handed rock track, but here it has a new wave flavour evocative of The Cars's classic first album. A clever vocal arrangement is allied to a slick, bass-led pop-rock riff featuring guitar from Joe Perry and Richie Ranno of the cult rockers Starz.

■ True Confessions

This pop-soul number could be mistaken for a Peter Criss solo song were it not for the weird choral section (performed by the wonderfully-named Azusa Cirtus College Choir) that Simmons slips into the middle of the song. Helen Reddy sings over honky-tonk piano on the chorus.

■ Living In Sin

In an early example of product placement in the entertainment industry, the Holiday Inn chain must surely have benefited from continual plugging in the song's tongue-in-cheek chorus. Aside from the cover of "When You Wish Upon A Star", this is the only song on the album not written by Simmons alone. He shares the credit with Sean Delaney and Howard Marks. Simmons begins the song speaking in a low tone of filthy letters sent to him by a fan. An invitation to his hotel room quickly follows, resulting in the mid-song phone conversation. Cher and Bob Seger guest on this track.

■ Always Near You/Nowhere To Hide

Kiss's much-maligned concept album (Music From) The Elder is foreshadowed in this complex piece. In fact, Simmons's gentle vocal at the beginning of "Always Near You" is echoed in two of The Elder's tracks, "A World Without Heroes" and "Under The Rose". Again, the Azusa Cirtus College Choir is employed on "Nowhere To Hide" as Simmons sings, impressively, in falsetto. Once more, the influence of The Beatles is evident as Simmons blends two songs into one whole as Paul McCartney did rather more ambitiously on The Beatles's classic Abbey Road.

■ Man Of 1000 Faces

With this song and the following "Mr. Make Believe", Simmons frames some of his most intriguing, adult lyrics in classic 60s-influenced pop arrangements. To Kiss fans who had only seen Simmons in demon make-up, "Man Of 1,000 Faces" had added mystery.

Howard Johnson: "It feels very 60s. People will laugh at this, but I think it's got a slight smidgeon of attempting to be Brian Wilson. Now I'm not for one minute suggesting that he succeeded, but there's a lot of orchestration. It's weird, very off-beat pop."

Dante Bonutto: "I think this song was about Lon Chaney. It's a great track and I love the big production on the whole record."

■ Mr. Make Believe

A lovely pop tune with a sorrowful lyric, "Mr. Make Believe" is a world apart from the braggadocio of "Calling Dr. Love". Even the mighty God Of Thunder, it seemed, had some small amount of doubt in his heart.

■ See You In Your Dreams

A remake of a song which appeared on Kiss's Rock And Roll Over two years previously. Here, Simmons improves the chorus with soulful female backing vocals and Cheap Trick's oddball guitarist Rick Nielsen gives the rocking riff a twist of simple old-fashioned rock'n'roll fun.

■ When You Wish Upon A Star

Unquestionably the maddest song ever recorded under the Kiss banner. With a mixture of heartfelt pathos and sly humour, Simmons sings this romantic standard accompanied by members of the New York and Los Angeles Philharmomic Orchestras. Walt Disney Christmas specials would never sound the same again.

Dave Reynolds: "The great man is slightly off key on this rendition of "When You Wish Upon A Star", but it's great!"

PETER CRISS

Rhythm and blues and 50s rock'n'roll were the great passions of Peter Criss's youth and these are the influences which inform much of the Kiss drummer's solo album. Criss recorded the album at New York's Electric Lady studios with producer Vini Poncia, who would subsequently work on Kiss's most pop-oriented records, *Dynasty* and *Unmasked*. The result was a lightweight, middle-of-the-road pop album which ultimately sold the least of all the Kiss solo efforts.

■ I'm Gonna Love You

The first of six songs on the album written by Peter Criss and Stan Penridge, the team who penned the classic Kiss ballad "Beth", Criss's signature song. "I'm Gonna Love You" is a rollicking opener, a swinging rock'n'roll number featuring soulful backing vocals and a brass arrangement inspired by the Memphis soul sound popularised by Al Green. Criss's vocals might not have the authority of Paul Stanley's, but he certainly knows how to work a tune.

■ You Matter To Me

Having had a huge radio hit with "Beth", Criss sticks to the middle of the road with this piece of pop fluff written by producer Vini Poncia with John Vastano and Michael Morgan. An extremely dated keyboard sound lends the song something of a 70s period charm, and the classic rhyme of "lovin" and "oven" would later be reprised on Marvin Gaye's "Sexual Healing".

■ Tossin' And Turnin'

Previously a hit for The Ivy League in 1965, this old-fashioned rocker is delivered in the style of Kiss circa Love Gun. Criss has a lot of fun with the lead vocal, sparring with female backing singers. Possibly the corniest song ever recorded under the Kiss banner, the song is the sound of Peter Criss doing what he loves best. Some great cowbell sound, too.

■ Don't You Let Me Down

This Criss/Penridge smoocher has a hint of Ben E King's "Stand By Me" and a cheesy synthesizer sound that wouldn't be out of place on a Barry Manilow song. For all that, it's a sweet little tune confirming Criss as the soppiest man ever to play drums in a heavy metal band.

■ That's The Kind Of Sugar Papa Likes

Mixing elements of 50s rock'n'roll with 70s glam rock, this daftly-titled Criss/Penridge song evokes images of 70s partygoers dancing badly with their thumbs hooked in the belt loops of their jeans. Toto's Steve Lukather contributes a very good guitar solo.

Rudy Reed: "There's a guy called Chris Cross and it's like that. A dreadful AOR/MOR track."

■ Easy Thing

Oddly, Peter Criss does not play drums on three of the songs on his solo album, leaving it to session man Alan Schwartzberg. On "Easy Thing", another Criss/Penridge composition, Criss puts all his energy into a melodramatic lead vocal delivered over cooing backup vocals and soft strings.

■ Rock Me Baby

Although written by Sean Delaney, "Rock Me Baby" is effectively "I'm Gonna Love You Part II", a jiving rock'n'roller with soul overtones.

■ Kiss The Girl Goodbye

A pretty ballad sung delicately by Criss over acoustic guitars played by Stan Pendridge, "Kiss The Girl Goodbye" is this album's "Beth". Criss and Penridge wrote the song, and in a cheeky reference to the drummer's day job, the first word of the title is printed in the Kiss logo.

■ Hooked On Rock'n'Roll

Steve Lukather helps out again with a guitar solo as Criss hams it up on this rock/soul number written with Penridge and Vini Poncia.

Kiss visit Buckingham Palace

■ I Can't Stop The Rain

"This is New York," Criss's voice echoes at the start of this gentle piano-led ballad, written by Sean Delaney. Again, there are echoes of "Beth" as Criss sings of heartache and loneliness over a lush orchestral backing. The album has been roundly dismissed by critics and even by many Kiss fans, but this song might have provided Kiss with another MOR hit.

Kiss in 1978: within a year, the smiling Peter Criss would be out of the band

DOUBLE PLATINUM

Kiss's first greatest hits album, this twenty-track collection features all of the group's classic tracks from 1974–77, plus a new version of "Strutter", titled "Strutter '78", as a lure for avid Kiss collectors. *Double Platinum* was released in 1978 to mark time while the band recorded *Dynasty*.

Tracklisting: "Strutter '78", "Do You Love Me", "Hard Luck Woman", "Calling Dr. Love", "Let Me Go Rock 'N' Roll", "Love Gun", "God Of Thunder", "Firehouse", "Hotter Than Hell", "I Want You", "Deuce", "100,000 Years", "Detroit Rock City", "Rock Bottom", "Rock And Roll All Nite", "Beth", "Makin' Love", "C'mon And Love Me", "Cold Gin", "Black Diamond".

Howard Johnson: "It's funny to be able to say ''78' instead of just 'Strutter'. I love the opening line, 'I know a thing or two about her,' over that plodding drum beat. Irresistible plod! *Double Platinum* was great because you got your own platinum disc, which was so appallingly bad. It was seven-inch as well, which was no good. At least make it a fucking album! It was really cheap piece of card coloured silver, but it was your own platinum disc signed by Kiss."

DYNASTY

The most controversial record of Kiss's career, *Dynasty* was created under huge internal pressure as drummer Peter Criss was effectively ousted from the band in favour of session player Anton Fig, who had performed so impressively on Ace Frehley's solo album. Criss features on just one of *Dynasty*'s nine tracks, his own composition "Dirty Livin'", on which he also sings the lead vocal. Although he appeared on the cover of this album and the next, *Unmasked*, Criss left Kiss at the end of the *Dynasty* tour. However, for fans unaware of the gravity of Criss's problems within the band, the controversy centred on the first single issued from *Dynasty* – the disco-influenced "I Was Made For Lovin' You".

Dynasty was released on May 23, 1979 and was soon certified double platinum. But on the ensuing tour, Criss's disillusionment was manifested in a series of below-par performances. *Dynasty* is a maligned album, not just by diehard fans but by Gene Simmons, who has continually voiced his displeasure over the lightweight nature of the music. But for Paul Stanley, it remains a vindication of his pop songwriting skills. Moreover, in the age of disco and New Wave, Kiss had to progress or risk being written off as 70s rock dinosaurs. For all of Gene Simmons' reservations about *Dynasty*, the album actually kept Kiss alive.

■ I Was Made For Lovin' You

In the 1999 movie *Detroit Rock City* – set in the 70s, starring and inspired by Kiss yet not technically "a Kiss movie", as Paul Stanley has stressed – a group of teenage Kiss fans express their hatred of disco music and confidently declare: "Kiss would never make a disco song." The joke, of course, is that Kiss did exactly that in 1979 with "I Was Made For Lovin' You". Written by Paul Stanley with producer Vini Poncia and songsmith Desmond Child (later the author of hits by Aerosmith, Bon Jovi and Cher), "I Was Made For Lovin' You" was inspired by Stanley's visits to legendary New York nightclub Studio 54. Many Kiss fans were horrified by the song's unapologetic disco groove, but "I Was Made For Lovin' You" provided Kiss with a world-wide hit and was reworked as an out-and-out rock song on the reunion tour some twenty years later.

Howard Johnson: "Brilliant song. Really camp disco. Really old-fashioned sounding synthesizer. An astonishingly good combination of rock and disco. You'd expect it to be totally shit, wouldn't you? I saw them do it live at Bingley Hall and it was appalling: tub-thumping go-go in a cattle shed. Useless!"

Andy Hunns: "At Sunderland Mayfair, the DJ always used to play 'I Was Made For Lovin' You'

The Rolling Stones, whose "2000 Man" was covered by Kiss on Dynasty

because it was the only Kiss song that girls danced to. You could get up and do your stuff to Kiss and the dancefloor would be full of nice women. It was one for the girls, but ultimately more for the boys."

Graham Stroud: "When I saw Kiss on the farewell tour in America they played 'I Was Made For Lovin' You' and they made a big thing out of introducing it because the audience over there is a real rock following – disco sucks and all that. They got slaughtered for this song and Kiss fans are still divided over it. Whether you like this song or not determines what kind of a Kiss fan you are. When they played it live they metaled it up and it sounded like any other Kiss song, but there's two ways of looking at it. They had the balls to write it and risk alienating their fans, but being cynical, you could say that they were chasing the dollar because disco music was so big at the time. I remember buying the 12-inch single and being disappointed that it was no different from the album version. But they had to do a disco song – Rod did!"

Tony Cooke: "All I ever wanted to do was meet Paul Stanley and I did so at Wembley in 1997. I was a punter, I'd paid for my tickets, and I was with two lads who I'd grown up with who were massive Kiss fans. As we were walking out, the girl who was doing the guest list shouted my name and gave us passes for the aftershow party. Another girl who knew me grabbed my hand and introduced me to Gene Simmons. I didn't know what to say to him. I tried to think of something interesting to say, so I told him that the version of 'I Was Made For Lovin' You' they played that night was crap. They pumped it up. It was like Rage Against The Machine. And Gene said he agreed. Then Paul walks in the bar and Gene calls him over. Gene told him what I'd said and Paul is standing there gobsmacked. They had a row! I just held my programme out for them to sign and then crept away."

■ 2000 Man

The self-appointed "Hottest Band In The World" covers the self-appointed Greatest Rock 'N' Roll Band In The World: Kiss plays the Rolling Stones.

Just about every rock band on the planet has been influenced in some way by the Stones, and Kiss paid tribute by re-interpreting Jagger and Richards' "2000 Man", from the Stones's bizarre, acid-inspired 1967 album *Their Satanic Majesties Request*. Originally a quirky '60s pop period-piece, Kiss transform the song into a driving hard rock number, its strange, dehumanised lyrics sung with cool detachment by Ace Frehley.

■ Sure Know Something

On his solo album, Paul Stanley was just warming up for "I Was Made For Lovin' You" and this brilliant pop rock song. "Sure Know Something" was *Dynasty*'s second single, its slick arrangement and irresistible melody making it an obvious choice. Gene Simmons might have hated playing the funky bassline, but no matter: this song is all about Paul Stanley.

Howard Johnson: "It's a genuinely great song. I like Paul's falsetto in the verses. Clearly, Studio 54 was still rocking New York. Paul was there for the lifestyle and Gene was there for the cash. A great tune and truly useless lyrics: 'I've been a gambler but I'm nobody's fool and I sure know something'. Well, what? What do you know? I didn't know what the something he knew was."

Leigh Marklew: "*Dynasty* brought a change within Kiss and probably marked the real end of the original line-up and the very best years. Who drummed on this album? Who was fucked up? When you hear tracks like this it doesn't really matter. 'Sure Know Something' really is one of the best pop songs I've ever heard, and one of the standouts from the *Unplugged* album that came much later. And on this song, Paul didn't have to copy what he was listening to every night at Studio 54, unlike another *Dynasty* fave we could mention."

Dave Reynolds: "The best track on *Dynasty* by a mile. I always remember the bit in the video where Paul motions to the star on his face while singing the line 'I've been starry-eyed'. A very cool song and one that sounded like it could've just as easily been on Paul's solo album."

■ Dirty Livin'

As the last recording made by Peter Criss before his departure from Kiss, "Dirty Livin'" is assured a place in the band's history. Remarkably, given his tenuous position in the group at the time, Criss delivers a fine, high-spirited performance as both drummer and singer. Like "I Was Made For Lovin' You", "Dirty Livin'" has a heavy disco influence and Criss's lyrics betray the fatigue – mental, physical and spiritual – resulting from his rock star party lifestyle.

■ Charisma

Gene Simmons is wrong about *Dynasty*. It's a great album. What's more, the two songs that Simmons contributed are far better than any he has written since the mid 1980s. "Charisma" has Simmons oozing dark sexuality over a taut rock riff: stronger, certainly, than the *Carry On . . .* double-entendres and metal-by-rote of his late 80s nadir.

Dante Bonutto: "This is my favourite ever Kiss song. It ought to be covered by somebody, maybe Robbie Williams would do a good job. That whole era of *Dynasty* and *Unmasked* has been much maligned, even by them, but I love the pop era and I don't think you should ever knock your own records."

■ Magic Touch

More classic power-pop from Paul Stanley, the driving force behind *Dynasty*. "Magic Touch" packs all the rock power of Kiss in a riff that smacks of Gene Simmons, but as on his solo album, Stanley's pop sensibilities come swiftly to the fore, especially when the band ease off the gas for a few bars and Stanley sings in fragile falsetto.

Howard Johnson: "Very fey but a really nice tune. I like some of the little refrains they put in there, which makes it very poppy. *Dynasty* and *Unmasked* are my favourite albums. It was a very short period in their history when I thought they were 'da bomb'."

Gary Banton: "This track hit me the first time I listened to *Dynasty*. It sounds so full and lush and I love the way the notes of the guitar chords are individually picked out."

■ Hard Times

Ace Frehley has written more celebrated songs than this – "Shock Me", "Cold Gin", etc – but "Hard Times" is one of his very best: an autobiographical tale of juvenile delinquency which struck a chord with millions of disaffected teens. Over a typically tough, spare hard rock riff, Frehley recalls a misspent youth filled with street fights, illegal drinking and arrests. "The hard times are dead and gone," the millionaire rock star concedes, "but the hard times have made me strong."

Dante Bonutto: "This is a fantastic track and I loved the fact that it was autobiographical. Frehley was doing two tracks per album by this time, and I always looked forward to hearing what he would come up with."

■ X-Ray Eyes

Having the extra-sensory superpowers of a comic-book hero comes in pretty handy, as Gene Simmons notes on "X-Ray Eyes". "I can see right through your lies," he sneers over the clipped harmonies. Whatever his reservations about *Dynasty*, both this and "Charisma" fit the album's mood perfectly.

Dante Bonutto: "This always reminds me of the Ray Milland film of the same name. I'm a big fan of the movie too."

Gary Banton: "Quite a dark riff on this one with Gene's bass leading the melody. The verse bass part actually reminds me of his part in the chorus of "Love 'Em And Leave 'Em", with its off-beat pulls. And it's great to hear Gene singing quite high in the chorus."

■ Save Your Love

His confidence boosted by the success of his solo album, Ace Frehley roused himself to write two tracks for *Dynasty*, although "Save Your Love" is in truth a bit of a dog, and certainly the weakest track on the album. Ace's cool indifference works on the verses but not even Paul Stanley can help the chorus.

The irony, of course, is that Kiss did not unmask with *Unmasked*. They would not do so for another three years - on the cover of their 1983 album *Lick It Up*. Instead, Kiss entered the 1980s with their greasepainted image intact but with their original line-up rapidly disintegrating.

4

THE 1980s & '90s

UNMASKED

Released in May 1980 and produced by Vini Poncia, Unmasked was the first Kiss album since 1975's Dressed To Kill which did not achieve gold status in the United States. This was despite the involvement of the veteran New York producer, who had already produced Peter Criss's solo album and Kiss's Dynasty, and had a track record which included Ringo Starr and the then-celebrated all-girl rock group Fanny.

On drums Unmasked featured Criss's session player replacement from Dynasty Anton Fig. Then, in Australia, where the band toured with their new regular drummer Eric Carr wearing fox-styled make-up, (as opposed to his predecessor's cat image) the album was a huge success. In fact Kiss recorded their biggest ever concert attendances on the Australian leg of the Unmasked tour.

■ Is That You?

"Oww!!" Paul Stanley gasps as Kiss begin a new decade in gloriously over-the-top fashion. Although written by outsider Gerard McMahon, "Is That You?" could easily pass for a Paul Stanley song.

Certainly, Stanley sings it as if it were one of his own. With its bubblegum metal style and bitchy lyric straight out of a school playground, "Is That You?" is one of the trashiest songs Kiss have recorded, and a spectacularly kitsch introduction to the album.

■ Shandi

Pure pop lovingly crafted by Paul Stanley and producer Vini Poncia, "Shandi" is the only single to be released from Unmasked in the US. "I Was Made For Lovin' You" cashed in on the disco boom and "Beth" seduced MOR radio, but "Shandi" is arguably the softest song in the Kiss catalogue, a sweet little tune beautifully sung by Paul Stanley.

Leigh Marklew: "A soppy Kiss song? Well, yeah, if you can believe it. This just reminds me of happy, sunny teenage days sniffing glue . . . er . . . I mean snogging round the back of the youth club."

Dante Bonutto: "Do you think they knew what a shandi was in England? Great track, though."

■ Talk To Me

Not since Bob Ezrin worked on Destroyer four years previously had a producer exerted so strong an influence on a Kiss record, and on "Talk To Me"

Vini Ponica even smoothed out a few of Ace Frehley's rough edges. Frehley's guitar sound is cleaner, his vocals more focused, the chorus much sharper than, say, "Shock Me". Frehley might have yearned to rock out a little harder, but "Talk To Me" still carried his unique stamp.

■ Naked City

Like *Dynasty*, *Unmasked* ranks among Gene Simmons' least favourite Kiss albums, yet "Naked City" is one of his finest songs. Co-authored by Vini Poncia, Pepe Castro and occasional Kiss session guitarist Bob Kulick, "Naked City" delivers classic Simmons hallmarks – creeping bass line, badass riff, dark lyrics – with a lighter touch. Simmons even tones down his Demon persona to sing with rare sensitivity, an approach later refined on "A World Without Heroes", from the next album (Music From) *The Elder*.

Leigh Marklew: "I know that *Unmasked* is not one of the band's highly rated albums, but for some reason I really like it. Okay, so it has a poppy production, but I think there's some bona fide Kiss classics on *Unmasked*. I love the atmospherics and depth of 'Naked City' – a definite departure for Kiss. Maybe a precursor for *The Elder*? I would have chosen 'Is That You?', but Marionette's version just walks all over it!"

Gary Banton: "I always think of 'Naked City' as a sibling to 'X-Ray Eyes'. The mood and the riff are familiar but the track easily stands on its own merits. Gene's bass cuts through nicely and his vocals sound great when, like in "X-Ray Eyes", he pushes them higher than normal in the chorus."

■ What Makes The World Go Round

Another Paul Stanley/Vini Poncia collaboration, "What Makes The World Go 'Round" is essentially "I Was Made For Lovin' You" Part 2, its high-energy rhythm and powerful melody leading to a disco-inspired instrumental break that suggested that Paul was still spending his nights off at New York's Studio 54.

Howard Johnson: "There's nothing wrong with

a pretty little tune. The keyboards on that album are very much of its time, and I like that."

■ Tomorrow

If one song sums up Paul Stanley's genius for power-pop, this is it. Again co-written by Stanley and Vini Poncia, "Tomorrow" combines slick hard rock with a truly inspired chorus that ranks among Kiss's very best. Cheesy 80s synthesizers and hand-claps add to the celebratory atmosphere.

Howard Johnson: "Die-hard Kiss fans might think this is a really lame choice, but clearly, this is what Paul Stanley genuinely likes. I think he enjoys singing bouncy, poppy, inoffensive, slightly gay-sounding rock. And why not?"

■ Two Sides Of The Coin

If Ace Frehley was losing interest in Kiss at the turn of the '80s, it didn't show in his songwriting. "Two Sides Of The Coin" is one of three songs the guitarist contributed to *Unmasked* – more than on any other Kiss record – and it possesses all the energy of Frehley's solo album, due in no small part to Anton Fig's astonishing, fast-handed drumming. Peter Criss will always be remembered as the definitive Kiss drummer, but Criss rarely delivered a performance quite as powerful as Fig's on this track.

■ She's So European

A co-writing credit for Vini Poncia explains the overt pop flavour of this song, but the lyric is all Gene Simmons. The girl in question is actually American but she has a sophistication that Simmons finds irresistible, even if she is something of a fake who speaks with an accent acquired during a week in St Tropez. "She's so refined," Simmons sighs, "is that her screaming?" Clearly, his idea of refinement differs from that of the average European charm school.

Dante Bonutto: "Tracks like this reflect Kiss's pop heritage. Simmons and Stanley are both big Beatles fans and you hear a lot of that in *Unmasked*. When he put his mind to it, Simmons's voice is very much suited to pop, but after this, he started writing songs in his sleep."

■ Easy As It Seems

Kiss go funk? "Easy As It Seems" wouldn't have given Kool & The Gang any sleepless nights, but it's certainly the funkiest of all Kiss songs, begun with a deft bass line from Gene Simmons and polished to perfection by Vini Poncia, who co-wrote the track with Paul Stanley. Over smooth cod-soul harmonies and crisp guitar chords, Stanley proves himself not just a great rock'n'roll singer, but a great singer, period.

■ Torpedo Girl

This Ace Frehley tune is one of the most bizarre that Kiss have ever recorded. The funky theme of the preceding "Easy As It Seems" is combined with Beach Boys-inspired harmonies as Ace recounts a dream in which he goes for a swim and encounters a vision of loveliness on the bridge of a submarine. If that wasn't ridiculous enough, "Torpedo Girl" also features the obligatory submarine sound effects and a comical shout of, "Come on – get your feet wet!"

Howard Johnson: "Absolutely hilarious. I really like it, though, despite the fact that it is awful. Stupid lyric: 'What the hell, I think I'll go swimming away.' It's just so insane. I couldn't imagine playing it to anyone else in the entire universe and having them think it's any good – not even Ace Frehley."

Chris Dale: "Being a bass player and someone who writes silly lyrics, I'm bound to like 'Torpedo Girl' as it's got the funkiest Kiss bass line and the silliest lyrics ever. The whole concept that you could go for a swim and find a submarine with a girl on the bridge – what on Earth was he thinking of? It's genius! Ace doesn't do songs about boffing birds. I think he gets too messed up along the way."

■ You're All That I Want

Unmasked ends with that rarest of things: a Gene Simmons love song. The riff has plenty of muscle, but it is surprising to hear the author of "Goin' Blind" play this simple lyric with such a straight bat. Simmons's infidelity is the stuff of legend, but when he sings "You're All That I Want", he sounds almost believable. Almost.

New Kiss drummer Eric Carr (bottom left) made his debut on (Music From) The Elder

(MUSIC FROM) THE ELDER

After *Unmasked*, Kiss aimed to restore their waning popularity in the United States with a return to the epic hard rock of their legendary 1976 album *Destroyer*. They hired *Destroyer*'s producer Bob Ezrin to help recreate that album's huge sound, but Ezrin immediately expressed dissatisfaction with the demos the group had recorded, including two songs, "Nowhere To Run" and "Partners In Crime", which would later surface on the best-of collection *Killers*. Ezrin urged Kiss to take the bold step of making a concept album, a concept which itself seemed outdated in an era when new wave and punk rock had made the overblown rock operas of the 1970s obsolete. Unsurprisingly, Ace Frehley voted against the idea but Gene Simmons and Paul Stanley relished the challenge. As a new band member, drummer Eric Carr had no say in the matter, although he faced a daunting challenge in making his recording debut for Kiss on a concept album of music which was alien to the band's past.

Simmons wrote the storyboard for the album: a mythical tale of a wise and benevolent order, The Elder, who select a young boy to rise up against a faceless evil which threatens mankind. A load of old tosh, perhaps, but it inspired some of Kiss's most adventurous music.

The public, however, did not take to the experimental nature of *The Elder*. The album sold so poorly that Kiss did not tour to support it. This prompted a drastic rethink and the departure of Ace Frehley, leaving Simmons and Stanley as the only original members of Kiss.

■ Fanfare

This is not a song but rather it's a brief orchestral introduction, composed by Paul Stanley and Bob Ezrin in a faux-medieval style. The piece is performed by The American Symphony Orchestra, which features throughout the album. *The Elder's* pompous tone is set, and a clear message is sent: this is no ordinary Kiss album.

■ Just A Boy

Over gently strummed acoustic guitars, Paul Stanley gets into character in pre-pubescent falsetto. The boy hero is pictured on a ship navigating a storm at sea. "Love Gun" this is not.

■ Odyssey

Featuring piano, strings and intricate vocal harmonies, "Odyssey" is *The Elder's* centrepiece and the most ambitious recording Kiss have ever undertaken. This grandiose mini-opera is so far removed from anything that Kiss had previously created, it is perhaps not surprising that it was written not by Kiss themselves but by an outsider Tony Powers.

■ Only You

After the rousing orchestral coda of "Odyssey", the abrasive rock riffing at the start of Gene Simmons' "Only You" comes as something of a surprise, as does a Simmons song without any reference to copulation. The song's hard-edged yet unorthodox pop-rock is more akin to Simmons' solo material than to his other Kiss songs. It also incorporates the refrain from "Just A Boy", evidence that Simmons and Stanley were in close collaboration throughout the songwriting process.

■ Under The Rose

Eric Carr co-wrote two songs on *The Elder* – an impressive feat given that Simmons and Stanley had written the bulk of Kiss's songs since the group's inception. It is was with Simmons that Carr created "Under The Rose", a portentous and rather bombastic rock epic. A huge choir adds weight to the booming chorus over a classic Simmons riff. In the verses, Simmons sings with a quiet authority later echoed on "A World Without Heroes".

Gary Banton: "Gene's singing is perfect on the lighter passages in this song. He really has a great tone and timbre to his voice. When the chorus comes in it is powerful and haunting and the choral vocal almost sounds spiritual in a Gregorian Chant kinda way. I guess that was the idea. Eric's drumming is thunderous and he also gets his first writing credit for the storming guitar riff he came up with here."

■ Dark Light

Beginning with a stuttering riff that brazenly rips off John Williams' creepy theme music to the film *Jaws*, the oxymoronic "Dark Light" is the most straightforward rock track on the album. Writing credits are shared by Ace Frehley, Gene Simmons, occasional stand-in drummer Anton Fig and rock legend Lou Reed, whose 1973 album *Berlin* was produced also by Bob Ezrin. Despite the unlikely

Lou Reed, an unlikely collaborator on **The Elder**

heard it for the first time on CD, I thought the actual song jumped and sounded generally odd. But no! I really like it now and I think it's wonderful how modern technology has opened up a whole new chapter in my life, while giving it a new meaning at the same time. Praise the Lord!"

■ The Oath

If fans worried that Kiss had lost their flair for hard rock, "The Oath" eased their fears. Over thunderous riffing that sets off at a gallop, Paul Stanley sings heroically and deftly rides the song's clever breaks. Stanley wrote the track with producer Bob Ezrin and Tony Powers.

Chris Dale: "It's got the big metal riff that we all love and a lyric about coming through a dream to an ancient door. Nobody could better that."

■ Mr. Blackwell

Not since "God Of Thunder" had Gene Simmons sounded so evil. Simmons wrote "Mr Blackwell" with Lou Reed, and sings it with wicked delight. "Mr. Blackwell" also boasts one of Kiss's most inventive arrangements: taut, ominous and led by Simmons' probing bass. If the lyrics offer few clues to the role of Mr. Blackwell in *The Elder*'s vague story, it hardly matters: as a piece of spooky rock drama, "Mr Blackwell" is one of Simmons's best.

Leigh Marklew: "Wooaahh! Back to that guttural, lurching, grinding Simmons trademark sound. A totally brilliant and weird song with an amazing swirling backwards guitar solo. It's also co-written by Lou Reed, which must be cool. Mustn't it?"

■ Escape From The Island

Ace Frehley and Eric Carr combined with Bob Ezrin on this frenetic hard rock jam. For Carr – the diminutive new kid on the block – "Escape From The Island" was an opportunity to show off his powerful drumming and establish himself as a more than capable successor to Peter Criss. For Frehley, it was a last hurrah before he quit the group. A wailing siren adds to the excitement, as on "Firehouse" and various other metal anthems,

combination of writers, Frehley's half-spoken lead vocal and flashy guitar solo point to the song's true inspiration. How Kiss would miss Ace's unique persona on subsequent albums.

■ A World Without Heroes

As Kiss's blood-dribbling, fire-breathing, groupie-boffing Demon and God Of Thunder, Gene Simmons is not renowned for his sensitivity, yet he sings "A World Without Heroes" in a tone of genuine, heartfelt sincerity. Again, Lou Reed helped in the creation of the song, along with Paul Stanley and Bob Ezrin. The song's romantic idealism and subtle beauty made it an obvious choice for a single.

Leigh Marklew: "I used to have this on *The Elder*, of course, but also on seven-inch picture disc vinyl, on which they sported dreadful bouffant hairdos and Kiss-meets-the-aerobics-teacher jumpsuits. Both versions I had were on horribly scratchy, poppy and jumpy vinyl. So until recently, when I

Judas Priest's "Breaking The Law", Saxon's "Freeway Mad" and Iron Maiden's "Sanctuary" among them. For metal bands at the turn of the 80s, the siren was an essential accessory.

■ I

If *The Elder* is Kiss's "serious" album, its closing track proved a curious mixture of conceptual gibberish and rollicking rock'n'roll. Gene Simmons and Paul Stanley hadn't traded verses on a Kiss song since the mid 70s, but they do so on this brash yet playful Simmons rocker. At one point Paul Stanley sings in the manner of Vegas-period Elvis Presley. There is also a mid-song break where massed clicking fingers echo Queen's "Crazy Little Thing Called Love". The chorus of "I believe in me" is exultant and the finish pure Hollywood hokum: heavy footsteps, a clanking door bolt, and the conversation between members of The Elder. "He has the look of a champion," one says. "A real champion." Who was the boy? What was his mission? Would he succeed? The questions remain unanswered. *(Music From) The Elder* is the soundtrack to a film that was never made – and the weirdest record that Kiss ever created.

Mark Taylor: "I'm one of those strange creatures who loves the whole of *The Elder*. I admired the sheer brass neck of changing from *Saturday Night Fever* disco to a Rush-style concept album. 'I' is so full of life and and a great song to jump about to in the heavy metal disco."

Dave Reynolds: "*The Elder* was a rather confusing concept album and very underrated. 'I' is a real anthem. A great song. I can't say the same for Kiss's image at the time. That short-haired Studio 54 look was NOT what Kiss was about. I think many fans felt they'd made a big mistake. Reading photographer Barry Levine's comments in his Kiss book reveals that even some closest to the band thought they were nuts too."

Kiss, 1981: (left to right) Eric Carr, Ace Frehley, Paul Stanley, Gene Simmons

Killers *album cover shoot, 1982*

KILLERS

A UK-only 1982 release that preceded the next legitimate Kiss album *Creatures Of The Night* by five months and helped restore the band's reputation as a hard rock act following the confusion which greeted the prvious year's *(Music From) The Elder*. Four new tracks, produced by Michael James Jackson, are featured alongside Kiss classics like "Love Gun", "God Of Thunder" and the definitive live version of "Rock And Roll All Nite".

Tracklisting: "I'm A Legend Tonight", "Down On Your Knees", "Cold Gin", "Love Gun", "Shout It Out Loud", "Sure Know Something", "Nowhere To Run", "Partners In Crime", "Detroit Rock City", "God Of Thunder", "I Was Made For Lovin' You", "Rock And Roll All Nite"(live).

■ I'm A Legend Tonight

A throwback to the uncomplicated pop rock of *Dynasty* and *Unmasked*, this Paul Stanley/Adam Mitchell number marks a return to simple values after the grandeur of *The Elder*. "I'm A Legend Tonight" is modern rock anthem with no frills save for some subtle harmonies on the chorus. Michael James Jackson's sparse production offers no clues to the thunderous new sound of the forthcoming *Creatures Of The Night*.

Chris Dale: "There's a story about a whole missing album circa 1981. That's the Holy Grail, isn't it? The pop of *Unmasked* and the heaviness of *Creatures Of The Night*. The four new tracks off *Killers* come close – really heavy and tuneful."

■ Down On Your Knees

Benefiting from a raw production, "Down On Your Knees" is a real old-fashioned stomper in which Paul Stanley demands all manner of mucky business from a girl who's alright because she's all he's got tonight. Stanley shares a writing credit with Mikel Japp and Bryan Adams, who would also contribute to the *Creatures Of The Night* album.

Chris Dale: "Obviously we love AC/DC but we don't need to hear Kiss trying to do that."

■ Nowhere To Run

Beginning with a resonating powerchord that recalls The Who's classic "Won't Get Fooled Again", this Paul Stanley track is the best of the four new songs on this collection. A gentle midsection, sung falsetto, echoes *Dynasty*'s "Sure Know Something".

■ Partners In Crime

A thinly disguised take on Foreigner's "Hot Blooded", "Partners In Crime", written by Paul Stanley and Adam Mitchell, is the weakest of the new tracks. The riff plods along uneventfully and the chorus is frankly pathetic. Stanley actually sounds bored as he sings it – which is incredible, given his reputation as one of rock 'n' roll's most charismatic performers.

CREATURES OF THE NIGHT

In 1982, Kiss had a problem. To revitalize their career after the commercial disappointment of *Unmasked* and *(Music From) The Elder*, they intended to make their heaviest album to date, but their rocker-in-chief, guitarist Ace Frehley, had quit the group. Convinced that they could persuade Frehley to rejoin, Kiss enlisted the services of severa session guitarists including the ever-reliable Bob Kulick and newcomer Vincent Cusano. At the Record Plant studios in Los Angeles, Kiss set to work with producer Michael James Jackson. The result was an explosive new Kiss sound far removed from the rock'n'roll of the early albums and the slickness of *Dynasty* and *Unmasked*. In short, *Creatures Of The Night* is a definitive early 80s metal album built around an astonishingly loud drum sound. The guitar playing was fast and full of tricks: a world apart from Ace Frehley's loose, raw style. Frehley appeared on the cover of the album but his refusal to tour again with Kiss resulted in the appointment of Cusano – now named Vinnie Vincent – as the band's new guitarist. Vincent wore make-up styled on an Egyptian ankh design as Kiss unveiled their new tank stage-set on a tour of South America, during which they played before audiences of 200,000.

■ Creatures Of The Night

The album's title track – which was written by Paul Stanley and Adam Mitchell – provided a stunning introduction to the powerful new Kiss sound. Beginning with a deafening blast from Eric Carr, "Creatures Of The Night" is an all-out attack, with Stanley spitting doomy lyrics over strafing guitars.

Andy Hunns: "The heaviness – fuck me! Ace had gone and Peter had gone, but it was great. I've got the seven-inch single – it's pink. I used to love getting up on the floor at the Sunderland Mayfair for that one. I was looking a bit glammy, but not too much, maybe a little bit of eyeliner. And those little ankle-length Robin Hood boots. Good God!"

Dave Reynolds: "I heard this for the first time when Sir Geoff Barton premiered it while standing in for Tommy Vance on the *Friday Rock Show* on Radio 1. It was a relief to hear that Kiss had reverted back to being a heavy metal band again. The huge production job by Michael James Jackson still stands out today, with a lot of emphasis on Eric Carr's John Bonham-esque drumming. With this album, Kiss were back."

■ Saint And Sinner

This Gene Simmons song – co-authored by Mikel Japp – is full of his usual bragging, but after the tumult of "Creatures Of The Night", "Saint And Sinner" benefits from a looser groove which lends a casual authority to Simmons's sneer: "Kiss my heart bye-bye." The track also has a melodic quality absent in much of Simmons' 80s output.

■ Keep Me Comin'

One of Paul Stanley's funniest double entendres, "Keep Me Comin'" is all sexual rough and tumble in which Stanley whips himself up into a state of borderline hysteria. Again, Adam Mitchell has a co-writing credit.

Eric Carr: a little man who made a big noise

Chris Dale: "I was pretty young and hadn't heard Led Zeppelin, so when I got heard 'Keep Me Comin'' I thought it was amazing. What a great idea: this huge drum sound and these chugging guitars. Now I realise where it came from. I saw Kiss play Zeppelin's 'Whole Lotta Love' on the *Animalize* tour."

■ Rock And Roll Hell

Although a stereotypical Simmons plodder, "Rock And Roll Hell" is one of two tracks on the album co-written by Canadian rock superstar Bryan Adams and his longtime collaborator Jim Vallance. Adams was at this point a cult artist still two years away from his international breakthrough with *Reckless*. "Rock And Roll Hell" is a mighty, down-beat yet anthemic track, a run-of-the-mill tale of teenage misery and salvation in rock music. The style is so typical of Simmons, it's a mystery that he required extra input in its writing.

Chris Dale: "The whole *Creatures* . . . album brings back brilliant teenage memories. After I'd gotten into Kiss, this was the first new Kiss album I bought. And listening to the chorus of 'Rock And Roll Hell' while doing my homework was probably one of the turning points in my life. I sat there thinking, Maybe I don't want to go to college and get a job!"

Gary Banton: "From the opening riff and the thunderous tom toms you know that this is gonna be a Kiss epic! As the sound strips down for the verse it leaves just Eric's drums and Gene's bass, which has possibly the best Gene bass tone ever laid down on record! It really grinds and growls. A great anthemic chorus with Gene's vocals at full pelt and another atmospheric Vinnie solo complete this track."

■ Danger

For all its urgency, "Danger" is all bluster, a throw-away track written by Paul Stanley and Adam Mitchell. While the album's title track proved that Stanley could write brilliant heavy metal songs, "Danger" proves that nevertheless he's not always on the money.

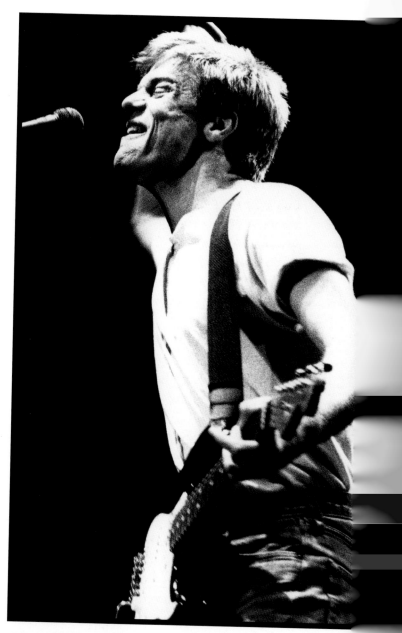

Bryan Adams: co-writer on two Kiss anthems

■ I Love It Loud

Kiss have recorded some bozo anthems in their thirty-year career, but none as idiotically brilliant as "I Love It Loud", one of three songs on *Creatures Of The Night* co-written by new guitarist Vinnie Vincent. Gene Simmons sings lead vocal but it is Paul Stanley who wrote the song with Vincent. Like "God Of Thunder", Stanley wrote the song with Simmons in mind. The stomping rhythm is perfectly suited to Simmons's stage persona, and only Gene could deliver a pretend-dumb line like "Whiplash, heavy metal accident" with the requisite deadpan humour. "I Love It Loud" also features some extra loud speaker-rattling drumming from Eric Carr and a cheeky false ending. All in all, it's delightfully gonzoid stuff.

Joe Mackett: "It's a heavy metal anthem. When I was in college in Bangor they had a video jukebox in the pub and 'I Love It Loud' was on there. The video was brilliant: a kid watching Kiss on TV, then his dad's newspaper bursts into flames and it goes into Kiss playing live with the tank stage-set and Paul Stanley rolling around on the floor."

Graham Stroud: "The chanting: Slade had done it – every band did it. But Kiss made it their own. The lyrics are appaling but it's one of Gene's finest moments."

Dave Reynolds: "*Creatures Of The Night* wasn't one of Kiss's biggest sellers, but 'I Love It Loud' is still played during ice hockey games in the States to this day!"

■ I Still Love You

On an album as loud and metallic as *Creatures Of The Night*, a love song like "Beth" would have been totally misplaced, hence this mighty power ballad from Paul Stanley and Vinnie Vincent. Stanley certainly over-eggs the pudding here, but his pleading vocal is possibly the most emotive he has ever recorded, backed by a dramatic, thunderous hard rock arrangement. Power ballads got a bad name in the late 80s, but "I Still Love You" really did put the "power" into "power ballad". "Cathartic" is not a word normally associated with Kiss, but it fits the bill here.

Leigh Marklew: "Kiss's recorded output dipped alarmingly from this point in. Basically, they started to follow fashion instead of define it and ended up just another 80s hair metal band, but without the attitude of early Mötley Crüe or Guns N' Roses. But before it all went pear-shaped they released *Creatures Of The Night*, which contained some great, bombastic rockers, and none more so than this archetypal power ballad (to end all power ballads). The drums sound like they are 10 feet across and Paul Stanley wrings some real soul out of his voice for one last time before

the ridiculous years set in. So Kiss had pretty much ten years of great records, which is all that any band has ever been good for."

Tony Cooke: "Whenever I've split up with a girl, 'I Still Love You' was the one I'd play, standing in my bedroom in all my rock gear: spandex pants; black velvet boots with purple tassels; and a silver jacket that I'd saved up for weeks to buy. Even though I was a drummer, I'd stand there with my foot on the bed playing air guitar to 'I Still Love You'. In my own little heavy metal world, I've got a lot of passion and emotion and this is the kind of song that brings it out in me. It's all about emotion. I'd play this for a week and then get back down the rock club, get pissed and meet someone else. That's what it's all about."

Gary Banton: "It's an often overlooked classic rock ballad. Paul's vocals are really heartfelt on this one and I'm sure many of us can relate to the sentiments he conveys."

Mark Taylor: "A sad song for moments of despair when I was separated from Miss Right – or, as it invariably turned out, Miss Right Now."

■ Killer

Gene Simmons and Vinnie Vincent collaborated on this mean and moody rocker. A twisting, darkly melodic riff adds to the threat in Simmons's vocal as he warns of a dangerous femme fatale. Gene Simmons scared of a woman? It's only a song, after all.

■ War Machine

The heaviest song on the heaviest Kiss album is the creation of Gene Simmons – predictably enough – and, more surprisingly, Bryan Adams and Jim Vallance. "War Machine" is very much in the vein of "God Of Thunder" and "Watchin' You": slow, mean, borne on a sinuous riff and heavy with foreboding. As the song grinds to a halt, Kiss's rebirth – a new band line-up with bold and brash new music – is almost complete. What followed was the most dramatic, hazardous and controversial decision of the band's career: the make-up was coming off!

Kiss unmasked at last: (left to right) Eric Carr, Gene Simmons, Vinnie Vincent, Paul Stanley

LICK IT UP

It was during a recording session at Right Track studios in New York City that Paul Stanley suggested to Gene Simmons that Kiss should take off their famous make-up. Stanley felt that it was time for Kiss to reinvent their image for a new rock era and to prove that they could compete with younger rock acts on a purely musical level. As Stanley saw it, the make-up was a hindrance which tied Kiss to the 1970s. Without it, they could begin afresh. With Vinnie Vincent now firmly established as a band member, Stanley was confident that Kiss could win over a new audience. Reluctantly at first, Simmons agreed. Despite his reservations, Simmons knew that with Ace and Peter Criss now gone, Kiss needed to move forward and shedding

the make-up would signify a new beginning and create huge interest in the group's new album.

Produced by Gene Simmons, Paul Stanley and Michael James Jackson, *Lick It Up* was released on September 18, 1983. The cover was simple: a photograph of the band in casual rock clothes, their faces exposed in public for the first time. Paul Stanley hardly looked any different without his Starchild mask. Gene Simmons poked out his tongue as if his imposing height and bulk were not enough of a clue to his identity. Many Kiss fans could not stop staring at the picture. Yes, they'd really done it.

Lick It Up became the first Kiss album to achieve platinum status in the US since 1979's *Dynasty*. Paul Stanley had been proven right: even without their world famous face-painted image, Kiss remained one of the world's premier rock acts.

■ Exciter

Picking up where *Creatures Of The Night* left off, "Exciter" is a high-energy metal track co-written by Paul Stanley and Vinnie Vincent. The latter contributed to the writing of eight of Lick It Up's ten tracks – more than either Stanley or Gene Simmons – and the effect was dramatic. Compared to Ace Frehley's rock'n'roll style, Vincent was a hotshot guitarist whose heavy riffs and spectacular solos brought the Kiss sound bang up to date.

■ Not For The Innocent

Described as "dour" by one UK reviewer, "Not For The Innocent" is heavy and atmospheric, sung by Gene Simmons, who wrote the song with Vinnie Vincent. "Lock up your daughters," Simmons drools. The God Of Thunder might have hung up his batwings and scary boots, but deep down he was still the same old sleazebag.

A rare shot of Gene Simmons' tongue

■ Lick It Up

Far and away the best song on the album, "Lick It Up" was a "Rock And Roll All Nite" for the MTV generation. Composed by Stanley and Vincent, its chugging, insistent riff, anthemic chorus and party mentality made it an instant Kiss classic and an obvious choice for the album's lead single. Surprisingly, it peaked at 31 on the UK chart, but "Lick It Up" remains one of Kiss's best-loved songs.

Joe Mackett: "It's the bozo-ness I love. It's also a great song when you're at that age when you're not having a great deal of sex but you'd like to be. When I was living in Wales, loads of people would say they hated heavy metal, but if you put 'Lick It Up' on the jukebox everybody's up and loving it."

Graham Stroud: "The make-up was off and they are ugly, but the video for 'Lick It Up' got a lot of airplay in the UK and they were huge throughout Europe. Vinnie Vincent was ugly with the make-up on! Take the make-up off and he's no oil painting! 'Lick It Up' is a great Kiss song and the best track on the album by a mile."

■ Young And Wasted

For all its pace and ferocity, this Simmons/Vincent number is one of several below-par tracks on the album. Paul Stanley helps lift the chorus but the verses are full of empty bluster from Simmons, as if he was trying a little too hard to prove that Kiss could duke it out with the new breed of metal bands.

■ Gimme More

After "Young And Wasted", another disappointment. "Gimme More" is a huffing, puffing, run-of-the-mill heavy metal song badly sung by Paul Stanley, who shares writing credits with Vinnie Vincent. Like "Young And Wasted", "Gimme More" is fast and loud but bereft of the style and melody that Kiss fans had come to expect from Paul Stanley.

■ All Hell's Breakin' Loose

Rapping on a Kiss song? The idea is as ridiculous as Judas Priest flirting with reggae on "The Rage", yet rap is what Paul Stanley certainly did on "All Hell's

Breakin' Loose" – to hilarious effect. The premise is highly unlikely: a "street hustler" accosts Stanley and asks him, "what be this?" and "what be that?", referring to the Kiss star's rock'n'roll clobber. Brushing him off, Stanley replies, "Hey man, I am cool, I am the breeze". It's pure comedy. The remainder of this Stanley/Simmons/Carr/Vincent composition is typical Kiss fare, with its thumping riff, shouty chorus and the rock-as-revolution lyric – but it's Paul's laughable hip-hop stance that makes "All Hell's Breakin' Loose" a truly extraordinary Kiss song, even if it is for all the wrong reasons.

■ A Million To One

As befits its title, *Lick It Up* is not an album that is rich in pathos, but Paul Stanley recreates the emotive power of his solo album on "A Million To One". Over a classy riff which was co-written by Vinnie Vincent, Stanley warns a departing lover that she'll never find another like him. Here, Kiss manage to ease off the gas for the only time on the album and the effect is stunning.

■ Fits Like A Glove

The first of two tracks written by Gene Simmons alone, "Fits Like A Glove" is all hammering heavy metal and aggressive sexuality, which Simmons pushes to an unpleasant degree when he boasts: "When I go through her it's just like a hot knife through butter."

Andy Hunns: "It's got a fantastic riff and Gene going, 'Oh yeah!' loads of times. 'Fits Like A Glove' said to me that Kiss had moved on from their pop rock to a bigger 80s sound with heavier riffs. I was a bit nervous about whether they could do it. It's a real get-your-head-down song."

■ Dance All Over Your Face

Gene Simmons can do much, much better than this. On future albums by Kiss he would be chastised by Paul Stanley for an increasing lack of commitment to the band, but on the evidence of this lacklustre track, the God of Thunder was already starting to get lazy.

Paul Stanley: "I am cool – I am the breeze!"

■ And On The 8th Day

Beginning with a flurry of drums and strident guitar reminiscent of The Who, this Gene Simmons /Vinnie Vincent anthem is even dumber than "I Love It Loud", but Simmons is making a serious point when he snarls "Legends never die!".

Graham Stroud: "Without doubt, this is one of the worst songs I've ever heard. The lyrics are dreadful, the tune . . . well, there's not really a tune. It's terrible. But it's the sentiment: 'And on the 8th day, God created rock and roll'. It's funny and there's no way they mean it. It's in the same ballpark as that song off *Psycho Circus* – 'I Pledge Allegiance To The State Of Rock 'N' Roll'. We know that rock 'n' roll is not the most important thing in the world, but we all love a song that's about plugging in, turning it up and banging your head. There are so many bands who mean every word they say, and you go, fuck off! Gene sings 'And On The 8th Day' with a straight face and you still piss yourself laughing."

ANIMALIZE

Kiss had re-established their rock god status with the million-selling *Lick It Up* and completed their first make-up-free tour, but all was not well within the camp. Gene Simmons had tired of guitarist Vinnie Vincent, whom he labelled arrogant and even miserly (in his autobiography *Kiss And Make-Up*, Simmons recalls Vincent inviting him out for dinner and then claiming he had forgotten his wallet, leaving Simmons to pick up the cheque). Simmons claims he had stayed loyal to Vincent when, in 1982, superstar guitarist Eddie Van Halen revealed an interest in joining Kiss. Simmons didn't know if Van Halen was entirely serious about his offer, and so declined. Now he was aggrieved to find Vincent challenging his and Paul Stanley's authority in Kiss. By 1984 Vincent was out and a new guitarist quickly drafted. Mark Norton was a highly technical player who had taught guitar in California. With his surname changed to the more rock'n'roll St John, he joined the group for the recording of a new album, *Animalize,* at New York's Right Track studios. However, before the band could begin a world tour in support of the record, St John fell victim to a rare illness, Reiter's Syndrome, which resulted in a swelling of the guitarist's hands, rendering him unable to play. After a problematic show with St John in a small theatre in Poughkeepsie, New York, Kiss hired their

Bruce Kulick joined Kiss for the Animalize tour in 1984

old friend Bob Kulick's brother Bruce as a touring guitarist. Mark St John attended several early dates on the tour with a view to resuming his role within the band, but to no avail. His condition did not improve and Kulick was made a permanent band member.

If Mark St John's illness had thrown a spanner in the works, even moreso did Gene Simmons when he accepted a role in the movie *Runaway*, in which he starred as a bad guy opposite the moustachio'ed *Magnum* heartthrob Tom Selleck. Simmons recorded vocals and bass for several songs before joining the movie shoot in Vancouver, leaving Paul Stanley to produce *Animalize* virtually single-handedly. Stanley's good friend Jean Beauvoir, formerly the mohicaned star of shock rockers The Plasmatics, played bass on a couple of tracks in Simmons' absence. Released in the final quarter of 1984, *Animalize* had been a struggle to make, yet its sales

Van Halen with Eddie Van Halen (second left)

matched those of *Lick It Up* and the accompanying tour with Bruce Kulick played to packed houses, beginning in the British seaside resort of Brighton on September 30, 1984.

■ I've Had Enough (Into The Fire)

Vinnie Vincent was not missed as Kiss kicked off *Animalize* with a replica of *Lick It Up*'s opening track "Exciter". "I've Had Enough (Into The Fire)" was co-written by Paul Stanley and Desmond Child, who collaborated on Kiss's 1979 smash hit "I Was Made For Lovin' You", although "I've Had Enough. . ." is a straightforward, frenetic metal track far removed from the disco-pop style of "I Was Made For Lovin' You".

■ Heaven's On Fire

The big hit single from *Animalize*, "Heaven's On Fire" is another Paul Stanley/Desmond Child composition and the best track on the album. Beginning with a spot of yodelling from Stanley, "Heaven's On Fire" is an anthem in the classic Kiss style. It also milks the oft-used "fire"/"higher"/ "desire" rhyming scheme.

Graham Stroud: "Probably the last great song they wrote. A crunching riff and Paul Stanley's voice on top form. They played it the first time I saw them live, so that's probably why I love it. It's metal but it's pop too."

■ Burn Bitch Burn

This rote Gene Simmons stomper is lifted out of the ordinary by a Paul Stanley-assisted chorus with echoes of "Firehouse", plus one of Simmons' most celebrated double entendres: "I'm gonna put my log in your fireplace."

■ Get All You Can Take

Paul Stanley has written some great rock'n'roll numbers in his time but this is certainly not one of them. It was co-authored by Mitch Weissman, and "Get All You Can Take" is rather like an irritating child: it makes a lot of noise when it's there, and it's a relief when it's gone.

■ Lonely Is The Hunter

A slow, grinding Gene Simmons number which struggles to make an impact. Perhaps Simmons' mind was already on the set of *Runaway*.

Under The Gun

The ill-fated Mark St John plays some fancy lead guitar as Eric Carr batters his kit in a fashion that would have given Peter Criss a coronary, but for all the fireworks, "Under The Gun" lacks a tune – surprising, given that its writers are Carr, Paul Stanley and Desmond Child.

■ Thrills In The Night

The second best song on *Animalize* after "Heaven's On Fire", "Thrills In The Night" is a definitive mid-80s pop-metal singalong led by an impassioned Paul Stanley. Stanley wrote the song with ex-Plasmatic Jean Beauvoir.

Dane Bonutto: "I interviewed Paul Stanley in the studio while Kiss were recording *Animalize* and Paul played me this track. He gave me a biscuit as well, a digestive. Simmons was away acting and Paul was producing the record. He was there at midnight, working alone. He was genuinely keeping the Kiss ship afloat. Someone had to be there and it was only me and him, and I wasn't contributing much. I ate one of his biscuits, tea as well. He could have gone mad. It was a bit surreal just sitting there with him."

■ While The City Sleeps

Never the strongest of Kiss albums, *Animalize* ends disappointingly with two tracks by Gene Simmons and Mitch Weissman. "While The City Sleeps" has Simmons bleating about "private wounds" and "cheap thrills". A throwaway track and an unconvincing performance.

■ Murder In High-Heels

An amusing title and funky riff make this track an improvement on the preceding "While The City Sleeps", but despite Simmons's cool delivery of the low-key hook, "Murder In High-Heels" ends the album not with a bang but with a whimper.

ASYLUM

Personality clashes had seen the Kiss line-up change dramatically since the start of the 1980s. First Peter Criss had departed, being quickly followed by Ace Frehley and then Frehley's replacement Vinnie Vincent. After Vincent, another guitarist, Mark St John, had been forced to retire from the group through illness. Throughout it all, founder members Paul Stanley and Gene Simmons remained united in their devotion to Kiss. However, by 1985 the once unthinkable was happening: a serious rift was developing between Stanley and Simmons.

The latter had secured his first Hollywood movie role in the thriller *Runaway* and was also beginning to build a business empire in Los Angeles with his label Simmons Records and a fast-growing management stable. Understandably, Stanley felt that Simmons's increasing extra-curricular interests were starting to have an adverse effect on the band. Simmons has since admitted that his head had been turned by his success outside of the band, and that without Paul Stanley's drive and commitment, Kiss might have split up at this time. Stanley, though, was no quitter. He had helped to make Kiss one of the biggest bands in the world and he was not ready to stop now.

With Stanley overseeing production, Kiss recorded *Asylum* in July 1985 at New York's Electric Lady studios, the scene of former glories in the 1970s. *Asylum* marked the recording debut of the new guitarist Bruce Kulick, who had replaced the ailing Mark St John on the previous year's *Animalize* tour. Due, perhaps, to Simmons's business activities, Kiss did not tour outside the United States in support of the album. Despite Paul Stanley's best efforts, *Asylum* remains one of Kiss's weaker albums.

■ King Of The Mountain

An explosive start to the album is provided by drummer Eric Carr, who flails at his kit with the ferocity of Led Zeppelin's legendary percussionist

Paul on the Asylum tour

John Bonham. "King Of The Mountain" was written by Paul Stanley with Bruce Kulick and Desmond Child, and Kulick gets his first chance to shine with some fluid lead work in the outro. However, it's Stanley who carries the song in his characteristic chest-beating fashion.

■ Any Way You Slice It

Simmons is in playful mood on this freewheeling rocker, co-written with Howard Rice. Again, Eric Carr is in bullish mood on a thumping mid-song break, and Simmons finishes on a light-hearted note with a staggered bar room-blues ending.

■ Who Wants ToBe Lonely

One of Paul Stanley's regulation mid-80s pop-metal tunes, "Who Wants To be Lonely" is one of the strongest songs on the album, as could be expected of a track co-authored by Desmond Child and Jean Beauvoir. Stanley gives it everything he's got, as if acutely aware that the future of Kiss is in his hands alone.

■ Trial By Fire

A melodic Gene Simmons number built on a deliberate backbeat from Eric Carr and chunky riffing from Stanley and Kulick. The latter gains a co-writing credit with Simmons, who states: "I'm gonna live my life the way I want to." In the context of his behind-the-scenes dispute with Paul Stanley, this remark seems pointed to say the least.

■ I'm Alive

Paul Stanley works a little too hard on this track co-written by Bruce Kulick and Desmond Child. Fast and furious, it simply sounds like a race to the finish. Stanley's sex-crazed lyrics are equally uninspired. There's nothing here he hasn't said better – and funnier – on "Love Gun", "Room Service", et al.

■ Love's A Deadly Weapon

The frantic pace continues with "Love's A Deadly Weapon". Simmons and Stanley collaborated on this track with Rod Swenson and Wes Beech, but despite the significance of the band's two big cheeses writing together, the results are definitely underwhelming. Fast songs have never been Kiss's forte, and here the sheer speed of the riff leaves Bruce Kulick struggling to conjure up a guitar solo of any style.

■ Tears Are Falling

This was *Asylum*'s big hit single. The fact that Paul Stanley wrote it comes as no surprise, given Stanley's track record and the circumstances in which this album was made. "Tears Are Falling" is one of Stanley's sweetest melodies delivered over a pulsing riff that recalls the previous hit "Lick It Up". While Gene Simmons had his eye on Hollywood, it was this song above all else that kept Kiss afloat.

Graham Stroud: "Very pop. If you took away Paul's voice and let someone else sing it – for instance, Gene – it would be a horrible metal song. But Paul's voice lifts it. If Kiss didn't have the image they had, they might have had bigger hits with songs like this."

Dave Reynolds: "I thought most of the albums that Kiss released since *Dynasty* were extremely patchy – including *Creatures Of The Night* – especially those in the mid to late 80s where they found themselves competing with the likes of Bon Jovi and Mötley Crüe. There are really only a handful of songs I like (or even remember) but I loved 'Lick It Up' and 'Uh! All Night', the latter penned by Paul, Desmond Child and my old mate Jean Beauvoir. 'Tears Are Falling' is by far the best of the bunch and had a great video to encourage the MTV generation to buy the album. Bruce Kulick's guitar work also reminds me of some of the tones his brother Bob captured with his old band Balance in the early 80s."

Dante Bonutto: "I went to the video shoot neat the Tobacco Dock in London and the band allowed me to take their limo home, which impressed the neighbours – it was very big. They were staying at the Hilton and I got a ride back from there. I think I interviewed Paul over breakfast the next day and Samantha Fox was with him."

■ Secretly Cruel

The opening riff is reminiscent of *Rock And Roll Over*'s "Mr. Speed", but "Secretly Cruel" has none of that song's charm. It's a predictable routine workout for writer Gene Simmons right down to the S&M metaphor.

Led Zeppelin: Kiss paid their respects on "Radar For Love"

■ Radar For Love

There is hardly a rock band on Earth that has not been inspired in some way by the mighty Led Zeppelin, and Paul Stanley and Desmond Child pay tribute with this brash track. With its staccato riff and yelping lead vocal from Paul, "Radar For Love" is Kiss's answer to Zeppelin's "Black Dog". The sense of fun in the performance recalls the loose vibe of early tracks like "Nothin' To Lose".

■ Uh! All Night

If Paul Stanley was feeling the pressure of leading Kiss with minimal support from Gene Simmons, the strain doesn't show on Asylum's cheeky final track. Written by Stanley with Desmond Child and Jean Beauvoir, "Uh! All Night" is every bit as silly as its title suggests, but Stanley's joie de vivre is infectious. Like "Rock And Roll All Nite" with added sex, "Uh! All Night" is totally gonzoid, with chants of "Uh! Uh! Uh!" raising the comedy stakes.

CRAZY NIGHTS

Kiss got lucky with *Crazy Nights*. Having ignored Europe and other world markets on their US-only *Asylum* tour, the group then took a ten-month vacation but bounced back with the biggest UK hit of their career in "Crazy Crazy Nights", which peaked at number four in October 1987. Again, it was Paul Stanley's pop nous which provided a vital hit single, although Gene Simmons's songwriting would improve despite the distraction of his Simmons Records label launch.

Originally titled *Who Dares Wins*, the *Crazy Nights* album was recorded in Los Angeles with producer Ron Nevison, who had added a commercial sheen to Ozzy Osbourne's *The Ultimate Sin* a year previously. *Crazy Nights* was released in November 1987 and was followed by a comprehensive world tour which included special guest slots on the massive European Monsters Of Rock festivals. Before the UK Monsters Of Rock show at Castle Donington, where Kiss shared a bill with Iron Maiden, David Lee Roth, Megadeth, Guns N' Roses and Helloween, Kiss played an intimate warm-up gig at London's legendary Marquee club, where such rock legends as Jimi Hendrix, The Who and Led Zeppelin had made their name in the late 60s. Kiss's appearance at the Marquee also marked the relocation of the club to its final address on the Charing Cross Road. To quote *Spinal Tap* rockumentarist Marti DeBergi: "Don't look for it now, it's not there…"

■ Crazy Crazy Nights

Considered pure cheese by many diehard Kiss fans, "Crazy Crazy Nights" is the "Rock And Roll All Nite" of the 80s; anthemic, celebratory, more than a little goofy and one of the biggest hits of the band's career. Written by Paul Stanley and Adam Mitchell, its bubblegum pop style recalls the glam-rock of mid-70s Britain.

Joe Mackett: "I'd moved to London and was going out with a girl whose best friend was going out with a member of the Kiss Army. He had the white leather jacket with the Kiss faces painted on it. His girlfriend was into Kiss by association, whereas my girlfriend Helen liked the softer stuff like Bon Jovi. But when 'Crazy Crazy Nights' came out, that was one rock track that she'd always put money in the jukebox for."

Paul and Gene: laughing all the way to the bank with "Crazy, Crazy Nights"

Child have created some classic pop metal hits, but "Bang Bang You" is certainly not one of them.

■ No, No, No

Gene Simmons by rote. Co-authors Bruce Kulick and Eric Carr open up with all guns blazing at the start of the song, showing off their party tricks in the style of Van Halen, but "No, No, No" is little more than a vehicle for flashy musicianship.

■ Hell Or High Water

Crazy Nights saw Kiss aiming squarely at pop radio. Gene Simmons played along on "Hell Or High Water". Co-written by Bruce Kulick, it's one of the more accessible tracks Simmons created in the 80s, replete with a chanted chorus reminiscent of "I Love It Loud".

■ My Way

Not, sadly, a cover of the Sinatra standard (if you can just imagine it), "My Way" is a synthesizer-led pop number in the style of Van Halen's Sammy Hagar-era hit "Dreams". Composed by Paul Stanley with Desmond Child and Bruce Turgon, a longtime ally of Foreigner singer Lou Gramm, "My Way" is high-energy pop sung by a highly excitable Paul Stanley.

■ When Your Walls Come Down

If ever a song existed simply to make up the numbers on a Kiss album, "When Your Walls Come Down" is it. No amount of histrionics from Bruce Kulick can mask the banality of this track. As to why it took three people to write it, only Kulick, Paul Stanley and Adam Mitchell know the answer.

■ Reason To Live

Throughout the 80s the power ballad was the surest route to chart success for hard rock acts like Whitesnake, Poison and Heart, and "Reason To Live" is a classic example of the form, expertly crafted by Paul Stanley and Desmond Child. Stanley sings it from the heart and Bruce Kulick contributes some tasteful lead guitar. The chorus is

■ I'll Fight Hell To Hold You

Paul Stanley works hard on this uptempo rock track co-written with Adam Mitchell and Bruce Kulick, but for all his theatrics, he is unable to lift the song out of the ordinary. What came so easily on *Dynasty* and *Unmasked* – pop-oriented hard rock – now sounded like a struggle.

■ Bang Bang You

"I'll shoot you down with my love gun, baby," Paul Stanley exclaims with a nod to past glories. But "Love Gun" this is not. Paul Stanley and Desmond

Gene at Monsters Of Rock, 1988, on the Crazy Nights tour

a killer, but "Reason To Live" failed to match the chart success of "Crazy Crazy Nights", stalling at number 33 in the UK and 68 in the US.

Tony Cooke: "I am into the softer side of rock and this is a great power ballad."

■ Good Girl Gone Bad

With its chugging boogie riff and gruff vocals from Gene Simmons, "Good Girl Gone Bad" is redolent of ZZ Top, who at this point were still riding high in the charts after the success of the *Eliminator* album, their belated international breakthrough. Simmons, who wrote the track with Davitt Sigerson and Peter Diggins, drops the overt metal stylings of his recent material to create a more adult Kiss sound, a throwback to *Unmasked*'s "Naked City".

■ Turn On The Night

Like "My Way", "Turn On The Night" is a super-charged pop-rock tune heavy on the keyboards. Stanley wrote the song with noted hitmaker Diane Warren and sings it brilliantly, with Simmons adding a little grit on the chorus. Bruce Kulick's squeaky fills have left the song sounding rather dated, but this remains one of Paul Stanley's finest pop songs.

■ Thief In The Night

Producer Ron Nevison coaxes one of Gene Simmons's very best vocal performances on this stomping, funk-styled rocker. Simmons wrote the song with Mitch Weissman. It ends a patchy, lightweight album with a defiant blast of heavy rock.

SMASHES, THRASHES & HITS

Released in 1988, this greatest hits collection mixes classic 70s tracks with hits from the 80s. In a bizarre twist, "Beth" is re-recorded featuring vocals from Peter Criss's replacement Eric Carr. Two new tracks are also featured: "Let's Put The X In Sex" and "(You Make Me) Rock Hard".

Tracklisting: "Let's Put The X In Sex", "(You Make Me) Rock Hard", "Love Gun", "Detroit Rock City", "I Love It Loud", "Deuce", "Lick It Up", "Heaven's On Fire", "Calling Dr. Love", "Strutter", "Beth", "Tears Are Falling", "I Was Made For Lovin' You", "Rock And Roll All Nite", "Shout It Out Loud".

■ Let's Put The X In Sex

A typically saucy and flamboyant Paul Stanley anthem, co-authored by Desmond Child.

Joe Mackett: "Greatest hits albums usually have a couple of duff tracks thrown on there to get the fans to buy it, but this is actually a great song. I'd find myself walking down the street singing that ridiculous chorus."

■ (You Make Me) Rock Hard

Again, Paul Stanley and Desmond Child combine with Holly Knight on another typically tongue-in-cheek stomper.

HOT IN THE SHADE

Released in November 1989, *Hot In The Shade* was recorded at The Fortress studios in Hollywood, California, and produced the group's first top ten US hit for 14 years in the ballad "Forever". A weighty 15 tracks makes this one of the longest Kiss albums, if not one of the best. Sadly, it would prove to be Eric Carr's swansong. On November 24, 1991, Carr died of cancer in New York's Bellevue hospital.

Carr was last seen by Kiss fans on the 132-date *Hot In The Shade* tour, which featured another elaborate stage set based on the album cover's sphinx design.

■ Rise To It

A surprising start to the album with some blues-inspired slide guitar licks from Bruce Kulick leading into a typical Kiss anthem in which Paul Stanley assures potential willing partners that he is sure to rise to any occasion. Stanley wrote the song with Bob Halligan.

Gene and Paul rock Donington

■ Betrayed

A hard-hitting metal song with working man's blues lyrics spat out venomously by Gene Simmons. Simmons wrote the track with Tommy Thayer, the ex-Black 'N' Blue star who now works in the Kiss organization.

■ Hide Your Heart

Oddly, this song was also recorded by Ace Frehley long after his departure from Kiss. "Hide Your Heart" was written by Paul Stanley with Desmond Child and Holly Knight. The lyric is a tale of doomed romance and shady street characters, reminiscent of Barry Manilow's disco smash "Copacabana". With its big chorus and hooky riff, "Hide Your Heart" was an obvious choice for the album's first single.

Dante Bonutto: "It's a good song, and I don't remember many from the later albums. Ace Frehley's version was pretty good too."

■ Prisoner Of Love

Many of the songs written by Gene Simmons in the 1980s sound like they were casually knocked off with the bare minimum of effort, and "Prisoner Of Love" is one such song. Co-authored by Bruce Kulick, its bouncy riff is wasted on a what can only be described as a tired melody.

■ Read My Body

Funk metal was a big noise in the late 80s with bands like the Dan Reed Network and the Electric Boys. Kiss got in on the act with "Read My Body", in which Paul Stanley asks, "Are the letters big enough?" over a thumping cod-funk riff. Another Stanley/Halligan composition.

■ Love's A Slap In The Face

Further proof that Gene Simmons was operating on autopilot in the late 80s. On the *Crazy Nights* album he delivered "Love's A Deadly Weapon". Two years later it was "Love's A Slap In The Face". The song is as uninspired as its derivative title suggests; surprisingly so, given that its co-writer is Vini Poncia, the successful producer of Kiss's most pop-oriented records.

■ Forever

Again, it was Paul Stanley who produced the hit single that Kiss needed as they neared a new decade. Stanley wrote this classic rock ballad with AOR big-hitter and "King Of The Mullets", Michael Bolton. An impassioned vocal from Stanley and some tasteful acoustic guitar from Bruce Kulick saw "Forever" cruise into the US top ten.

Joe Mackett: "Completely different from their knucklehead rock-and-roll-all-nite stuff. A very good rock ballad. A power ballad."

■ Silver Spoon

One of the best rock riffs on the album is shot in the foot by a poor chorus. Writers Paul Stanley and Vini Poncia could and have done much better. Bruce Kulick does his best to enliven the song with some flashy lead work.

■ Cadillac Dreams

Another Gene Simmons song and another turkey. Again, Vini Poncia earns a writing credit, but on this album Poncia's pop touch deserts him. The riff harks back to the heady days of glam rock and the Sweet, but not even some tooting from the All Star Cadillac Brass can polish this particular turd.

■ King Of Hearts

Essentially a heavy metal version of "Hide Your Heart", penned by Stanley and Poncia.

Kiss: (from left) Paul Stanley, Eric Carr, Gene Simmons, Bruce Kulick

■ The Street Giveth And The Street Taketh Away

A pompous title for another throwaway. A Gene Simmons number co-written by Tommy Thayer.

■ You Love Me To Hate You

Paul Stanley works hard to inject some emotion into this song, but not even Desmond Child's assistance can lift the melody above the ordinary.

■ Somewhere Between Heaven And Hell

With a heavy riff reminiscent of Duane Eddy's "Peter Gunn Theme", "Somewhere Between Heaven And Hell" sees Gene Simmons and Vini Poncia attempting to recreate the magic of *Unmasked*'s "Naked City" to little effect.

■ Little Caesar

Gene Simmons's best contribution to *Hot In The Shade*, "Little Caesar" is a heavy boogie track co-written by Eric Carr and Adam Mitchell. For the only time on this album, Simmons creates a memorable chorus aided by some "whoah-ohs" from Paul Stanley.

■ Boomerang

With this Simmons/Kulick stomper, Kiss aim to end the album with a bang but raise barely a whimper. From Eric Carr's pummelling intro onward, "Boomerang" is entirely predictable save for Kulick's jazz-rock soloing. A certain candidate for "Worst Kiss Song Ever".

REVENGE

After the shock of losing Eric Carr to cancer, Kiss responded with their strongest album in a decade. The band found a new drummer in Eric Singer, formerly a star of Badlands and Black Sabbath and the first blond member of Kiss (although he would later dye his hair black when replacing Peter Criss on the 2001 Farewell Tour). They also reunited with Bob Ezrin. producer of the legendary *Destroyer* album, for the first time since 1981's *The Elder*. *Revenge* was dedicated to Carr's memory and saw Kiss revitalized and rocking harder than they had done since *Creatures Of The Night*. Preceded by a surprise hit single in "God Gave Rock 'N' Roll To You II", *Revenge* entered the UK chart at number 10 on May 23, 1992 and peaked at number six in the US in the following month.

■ Unholy

A new decade brought a new commitment to Kiss from founder member Gene Simmons. This is typified by "Unholy", a powerful opening track in

Eric Singer joined Kiss in 1992 following the death of Eric Carr

Spinal Tap: did Kiss rip them off?

which Simmons sounds once more like the God Of Thunder in his mid-70s pomp. Surprisingly, the song was co-written by ex-Kiss guitarist Vinnie Vincent, of whom Simmons is highly critical in his autobiography. "Unholy" combines the menace of "God Of Thunder" with the heavy metal sound of "I Love It Loud". Simmons's lyrics are the most intelligent he had written since *The Elder*, a welcome break from the boring sexism of much of his 80s output. Simmons had been coasting in the 80s, but *Revenge* saw him refocused. Indeed, "Unholy" is so strong that Kiss broke with tradition and employed this Simmons song as the album's opening track instead of a Paul Stanley song. If the preceding *Hot In The Shade* album suggested that Kiss were on their last legs, the sheer power of "Unholy" proved the band's validity in the grunge era.

■ Take It Off

Paul Stanley is in uproarious form on this swaggering rocker, exhorting girls to wave their panties in the air and, er, spread a little oil. A Stanley/Ezrin/Roberts composition, "Take It Off" is a stripper anthem in the style of Def Leppard's "Pour Some Sugar On Me".

■ Tough Love

After the thunder of "Unholy" and the sheer naked exuberance of "Take It Off", this Paul Stanley/Bob Ezrin/Bruce Kulick track is a disappointment. *Revenge* has some great moments but they're not to be found here.

■ Spit

There can't be a heavy metal band on the planet who hasn't seen their own life mirrored in the ultimate rock parody, *This Is Spinal Tap*. However, only Kiss have actually ripped off a Spinal Tap lyric for one of their own songs! Perhaps Paul Stanley was blissfully unaware of Tap's "Big Bottom" when he declared: "The bigger the cushion, the better the pushin'." Having written some of the most ridiculously sexist songs in rock'n'roll history, Kiss manage to surpass themselves on this absurd ode to the larger woman. Hats off to writers Stanley, Simmons and Van Zen.

■ God Gave Rock'n'Roll To You II

This reworking of Argent's 1970s rock anthem was originally recorded for the movie *Bill & Ted's Bogus Journey*. A Top Five hit in the UK, it features some of Paul Stanley's funniest ad-libs in a tumultuous climax. Argent's Russ Ballard (author of the Ace Frehley solo hit "New York Groove") shares writing credits with Simmons, Stanley and Ezrin.

Tony Cooke: "I wasn't happy with the *Bill & Ted...* association, because all these people who weren't Kiss fans started telling me how great this song is. I tried not to like it but now I love it. I was working in LA for a Janet Jackson single and my plane got delayed for a day. Everyone else was pissed off but I was delirious because that night Poison were playing with Cinderella, Dokken and Slaughter at the Universal Amphitheatre. Poison ended their set with 'God Gave Rock 'N' Roll To You' and 'Rock And Roll All Nite'. It is a massive rock anthem."

■ Domino

Two good Gene Simmons songs on one album? You're spoiling us! The growled vocals and boogie thump on "Domino" are vaguely reminiscent of ZZ Top's sleazier moments. Also notable is Simmons's musing over a "man-size predicament". It is, he notes, a big one.

■ Heart Of Chrome

A standard Paul Stanley chest-beater written with Vinnie Vincent and Bob Ezrin in which Stanley claims a lover sold tapes of their phone sex to the BBC. A joke, presumably.

■ Thou Shalt Not

If Stanley was treading water on "Heart Of Chrome", Simmons does likewise here, although Bruce Kulick chips in with an extraordinary guitar solo based on Grieg's *Hall Of The Mountain King* suite!

■ Every Time I Look At You

Paul Stanley sings sweetly over acoustic guitars on a tune that echoes Cat Stevens's "The First Cut Is The Deepest", which Rod Stewart took to number one on the UK chart in 1977 as a double A-side single. Paul Stanley and Bob Ezrin may well have heard Rod's version before writing this song.

Andy Hunns: "It's a really nice ballad. It's great on the *Unplugged* album. A love song. You've got to have one of those – if only just for the wife. I could have said 'Beth', but that would be a bit too predictable."

■ Paralyzed

Jewish heavy metal stars are not renowned for their funkiness, but Gene Simmons is shaking his not inconsiderable ass on this playful rocker, co-written with Bob Ezrin.

Paul shows his New York roots

Gene awaits "room service"

Eric Carr, 1950-1991

■ I Just Wanna

Reminiscent of "Heaven's On Fire", "I Just Wanna" has Paul Stanley in cheeky mood. Does he really say "fuck" on the chorus? It's all part of the fun. Another writing credit for Vinnie Vincent, this time with Stanley.

■ Carr Jam 1981

In tribute to their deceased bandmate, Kiss finished *Revenge* with this Eric Carr composition, a Led Zeppelin-inspired jam recorded in May 1981 when Carr was still new to the band. It is the only drum solo Eric Carr ever recorded.

ALIVE III

Kiss's live albums are the stuff of rock legend. *Alive!* provided a vital commercial breakthrough back in 1975 after disappointing sales of the band's first three studio albums. Two years later, *Alive II* confirmed Kiss's superstar status. Moreover, these two lavishly-packaged double-albums effectively defined the sheer excess of 70s rock. In 1993 the tradition was continued with the inevitable *Alive III*. The band once again enlisted Eddie Kramer, the producer of *Alive!* and *Alive II*, to work on the third instalment of this epic series. Kramer recorded Kiss's November 27, 1992 show at the Palace Of Auburn Hills in Michigan before a sell-out crowd of 9,880 fans. The band's set included modern Kiss classics like "Heaven's On Fire", "I Love It Loud", "Lick It Up" and "I Was Made For Lovin' You" plus a selection of older crowd-pleasers including "Detroit Rock City" and "Rock And Roll All Nite". The performances are spectacular and, once again, Paul Stanley's banter is a delight. "Every time we play this one," he says, introducing the hit ballad "Forever", "the place lights up just like a damn Christmas tree!"

Alive III was released in May of 1993 and peaked at number nine on the US chart and number 24 in the UK. A statement on the CD booklet states simply: "*Alive I, II* and now *Alive III* will be our testament, our monument to us, to you, and to the invincibility of rock'n'roll." *Alive!* and *Alive II* were tough acts to follow, but *Alive III* succeeded.

Tracklisting: "Creatures Of The Night", "Deuce", "I Just Wanna", "Unholy", "Heaven's On Fire", "Watchin' You", "Domino", "I Was Made For Lovin' You", "I Still Love You", "Rock And Roll All Nite", "Lick It Up", "Forever", "Take It Off", "I Love It Loud", "Detroit Rock City", "God Gave Rock'N' Roll To You II", "Star Spangled Banner".

MTV UNPLUGGED

MTV's live and informal *Unplugged* series has given a facelift to many older rock acts, and for Kiss *Unplugged* was the key to the long-awaited reunion of all four original band members. After 15 years apart, Ace Frehley and Peter Criss rejoined Kiss onstage at the end of an acoustic performance. The bulk of the set features the early 90s Kiss line-up of Gene Simmons, Paul Stanley, Bruce Kulick and Eric Singer, but the excitement generated by the introduction of Criss and Frehley convinced Simmons and Stanley of the validity of a full-scale reunion tour. If Kulick and Singer appear less than exhilarated in the photograph on the album's back cover, perhaps they realised already that their careers as a members of Kiss were about to end – albeit temporarily for Singer, who replaced Criss for the final leg of the 2000 Farewell Tour.

Released in March 1996, *MTV Unplugged* saw the most over-the-top rock act in the world working extremely well in an intimate setting.

Tracklisting: "Comin' Home", "Plaster Caster", "Goin' Blind", "Do You Love Me?", "Domino", "Sure Know Something", "A World Without Heroes", "Rock Bottom", "See You Tonite", "I Still Love You", "Every Time I Look At You", "2000 Man", "Beth", "Nothin' To Lose", "Rock And Roll All Nite".

CARNIVAL OF SOULS

As grunge revolutionised rock music in the 1990s, Kiss were cited as an influence by many of the genre's leading figures, from Kurt Cobain and his buddies in The Melvins to Pearl Jam's Stone Gossard and Stone Temple Pilots. Such admiration turned Kiss's heads and led to the disastrous decision to "go grunge" on *Carnival Of Souls*. As many observers have noted, Kiss virtually invented grunge with "Hotter Than Hell", but they could not hope to compete with the new breed of bands. Nevertheless, they downtuned their guitars and played in a style reminiscent of Alice In Chains. Bruce Kulick even sported grunge-friendly facial hair to match that of Gene Simmons.

Kiss in 1996: (from left) Gene Simmons, Bruce Kulick, Eric Singer, Paul Stanley

Carnival Of Souls was originally slated for release in 1996 but was shelved when the original Kiss line-up reunited at the expense of Kulick and Eric Singer. The album became a hot bootleg item before its eventual release in 1997, where it was subtitled "The Final Sessions".

■ Hate

With a heavy, downtuned riff which is redolent of the Seattle grunge icons Alice In Chains, this Simmons/ Van Zen/Kulick track makes a powerful opening statement. For all the controversy that surrounds these recordings, "Hate" is not too dissimilar to some of Simmons' songs featured on the *Revenge* album.

■ Rain

If Gene Simmons appears to relish the challenge of competing with the younger stars of the grunge movement, Paul Stanley sounds utterly out of sorts on "Rain". Credited to Stanley, Kulick and Cuomo, this boringly plodding number is frankly a bit of a racket, and completely lacking in the vitality of Stanley's classic material.

■ Master & Slave

Another Alice In Chains rip-off, this time from Stanley, Kulick and Cuomo. The title reeks of Simmons, who might have handled this dour song with greater authority.

■ Childhoods End

The first truly catchy tune, four tracks in on the album, written by Gene Simmons with Kulick and longtime Kiss affiliate Tommy Thayer. A stronger sense of melody recalls the grand design of *The Elder*. This is certainly one of the better tracks on the record.

■ I Will Be There

Another Stanley/Kulick/Cuomo composition in which Stanley sounds happier singing a pretty melody over acoustic guitars. The overall feel is reminiscent of the Alice In Chains "unplugged" albums *Jar Of Flies* and *Sap*.

■ Jungle

A semi-funky grunge-lite riff recalls Collective Soul's US hit "Shine". Paul Stanley wrote this with Kulick and Cuomo but again sounds unconvincing.

■ In My Head

Angst was never Kiss's strong suit, and this Simmons/Van Zen/St James track is all huff and puff. Very dull.

■ It Never Goes Away

Damned with faint praise, this is probably the best grunge song ever written by Paul Stanley, mostly because Stanley sings with a restraint befitting the slow dynamic of the music. Written by Stanley, Kulick and Cuomo.

■ Seduction Of The Innocent

No prizes for guessing this is the work of Gene Simmons. Over a riff that evokes images of Eastern bellydancers, Simmons sings the a husky tone which worked so well on *The Elder*. A success.

■ I Confess

Another throwback to *The Elder*, this Simmons/Tamplin song has Simmons singing the verses with quiet menace, but a heavy-handed chorus spoils the atmosphere. Nevertheless, a great solo from Bruce Kulick makes "I Confess" one of the stronger tracks on the album.

■ In The Mirror

With a little more of Kiss's usual gusto, "In The Mirror" could have been a success, but Paul Stanley sounds constrained by the grunge sound. Stanley wrote the song with Kulick and Cuomo.

■ I Walk Alone

Bruce Kulick sings lead on this, the album's best song, written by Kulick with Gene Simmons. Kulick's voice is spookily reminiscent of Ace Frehley's and the song sounds like an out-take from the Space Ace's solo album. All told, one of the weirdest songs ever recorded by Kiss.

PSYCHO CIRCUS

The first album by all four original members of Kiss in nearly 20 years. Peter Criss had appeared on the cover of 1980's *Unmasked*, but he had already quit the band before that album was recorded. Critics doubted that the original Kiss could put up with each other for long enough to make another album, but buoyed by the success of the *MTV Unplugged* set, the foursome went to work between January and April of 1998 and achieved, if not the impossible, then the implausible.

Produced by Bruce Fairbairn, whose previous credits included hit albums by Aerosmith and Bon Jovi, *Psycho Circus* was released in late 1998 as the Kiss reunion tour raked in millions around the world. In truth, *Psycho Circus* was a disappointment. All the elements of classic Kiss records were in evidence – arena-sized rock anthems, an Ace Frehley showcase and a slushy Peter Criss ballad – but the magic of those early records is missing. *Psycho Circus* was not the massive hit that Kiss might have hoped for, but the tour was a huge success.

■ Psycho Circus

The sound of a carnival barrel organ spirals eerily out of tune as Kiss unveil "Psycho Circus". Naturally, Paul Stanley is the ringleader and the band sound like they've never been apart. A classic curtain-raiser, written by Stanley and Cuomo.

■ Within

Ace Frehley reminds Kiss fans what they've been missing with some weird harmonics before this Gene Simmons track lurches into a heavy riff. A powerful, atmospheric track with more of Frehley's unique guitar stylings throughout.

Kiss reunited in 1998: (left to right) Ace Frehley, Gene Simmons, Paul Stanley, Peter Criss

■ I Pledge Allegiance To The State Of Rock'n'Roll

Boasting the silliest title of any Kiss song, this Stanley/Knight/Cuomo track is a natural successor to "Shout It Out Loud", with a pretend-dumb lyric that couldn't fail to raise a knowing smile among longtime Kiss fans.

■ Into The Void

A classic Ace Frehley rocker with a killer riff and spaced-out lyrics. When Kiss played their 3-D show, "Into The Void" was Frehley's showpiece.

■ We Are One

Gene Simmons recalls the pop sensibility of his 1978 solo album with this, the best track on *Psycho Circus*. Simmons sings with a sensitivity not heard since *Unmasked*. A clever arrangement and sweet harmonies make "We Are One" one of Kiss's very best pop songs.

■ You Wanted The Best

The rallying cry from *Alive II* is reprised in this thunderous rocker. Written by Gene Simmons, "You Wanted The Best" is reminiscent of the very first Kiss album, as Gene, Paul, Ace and Peter trade lead vocals in knockabout style. Ace's solo recalls the first track from that first album, "Strutter".

■ Raise Your Glasses

A ridiculous title given Stanley and Simmons's oft-stated distaste for alcohol and the weakest song on the album, written by Paul Stanley and Holly Knight.

■ I Finally Found My Way

If "I Pledge Allegiance . . " is essentially "Shout It Out Loud Part 2", "I Finally Found My Way" is the new "Beth", a soft, string-laden ballad crooned by Peter Criss but written by Paul Stanley and Bob Ezrin.

■ Dreamin'

Bruce Kulick might have been cast aside for the Kiss reunion, but he earns a writing credit with Paul Stanley on this powerful, anthemic rocker which carries echoes of Stanley's solo album.

■ Journey Of 1,000 Years

An epic closing track from Gene Simmons, with a grandiosity redolent of *The Elder*. Ironic that after years of failing to pull his not inconsiderable weight on Kiss albums throughout the 1980s, Simmons should write the two best songs on *Psycho Circus*.

BOX SET

November 2001 saw the release of the Kiss box set, simply titled *Kiss*, a lavish package featuring five CDs of Kiss classics and rare out-takes, some lifted from the unreleased album by Gene Simmons and Paul Stanley's pre-Kiss outfit Wicked Lester. The full tracklisting is as follows:

Disc One, 1966–1975: "Strutter", "Deuce", "Keep Me Waiting", "She", "Love Her All I Can", "Let Me Know", "100,000 Years", "Stop Look To Listen", "Leeta", "Let Me Go Rock'N'Roll", "Acrobat", "Firehouse", "Nothin' To Lose", "Black Diamond", "Hotter Than Hell", "Strange Ways", "Parasite", "Goin' Blind", "Anything For My Baby", "Ladies In Waiting", "Rock And Roll All Nite".

Disc Two, 1975–1977: "C'mon And Love Me", "Rock Bottom", "Cold Gin", "Watchin' You", "Doncha Hesitate", "Mad Dog", "God Of Thunder", "Great Expectations", "Beth", "Do You Love Me?", "Bad Bad Lovin'", "Calling Dr. Love", "Mr. Speed", "Christine Sixteen", "Hard Luck Woman", "Shock Me", "I Stole Your Love", "I Want You", "Love Gun", "Love Is Blind".

Disc Three, 1976–1982: "Detroit Rock City", "King Of The Night Time World", "Larger Than Life", "Rocket Ride", "Tonight You Belong To Me", "New York Groove", "Radioactive", "Don't You Let Me Down", "I Was Made For Lovin' You", "Sure Know Something", "Shandi", "You're All That I Want You're All That I Need", "Talk To Me", "A World Without Heroes", "The Oath", "Nowhere To Run", "Creatures Of The Night", "War Machine", "I Love It Loud".

Disc Four, 1983–1989: "Lick It Up", "All Hell's Breakin' Loose", "Heaven's On Fire", "Get All You

Can Take", "Thrills In The Night", "Tears Are Falling", "Uh! All Night", "Time Traveler", "Hell Or High Water", "Crazy Crazy Nights", "Reason To Live", "Let's Put The X In Sex", "Hide Your Heart", "Ain't That Peculiar", "Silver Spoon", "Forever".

Disc Five, 1992–1999: "God Gave Rock'N'Roll To You II", "Unholy", "Domino", "Every Time I Look At You", "Comin' Home", "Got To Choose", "I Still Love You", "Nothin' To Lose", "Childhood's End", "I Will Be There", "Psycho Circus", "Into The Void", "Within", "I Pledge Allegiance To The State Of Rock 'N'Roll", "Nothing Can Keep Me From You", "It's My Life", "Shout It Out Loud", "Rock And Roll All Nite".

The previously unreleased tracks are as follows:

■ Strutter

The first recorded version of the Kiss classic, as featured on the demo which secured the band a record deal with Casablanca. Produced by Eddie Kramer, this version features more upfront bass from Simmons and a looser feel to the guitars. Amazingly, "Strutter" began life as a Simmons tune called "Stanley The Parrot"!

■ Deuce

From the same demo as "Strutter", Simmons' vocal is softer than on the finished version of "Duece". This is Ace Frehley's favourite Kiss song.

■ Keep Me Waiting

A track from the unissued Wicked Lester album, recorded in 1971 and featuring Simmons and Stanley alongside Steve Coronel (lead guitar), Brooke Ostrander (keyboards), Tony Zarella (drums) and Ronnie Leejack (guitar). Written by Paul Stanley, it blends rock, soul, pop and folk in the manner of The Doobie Brothers.

■ She

Also from the unreleased Wicked Lester album, this is a very different version of the song that would later surface on *Dressed To Kill*. A flute intro recalls Jethro Tull and lush vocal harmonies are in stark contrast to the hard rock style of the Kiss version.

■ Love Her All I Can

Another Wicked Lester track reworked by Kiss on *Dressed To Kill*. Funkier and fuller-sounding than the simplistic Kiss recording.

■ Let Me Know

Originally titled "Sunday Driver", this is a rough demo version of the song from the first Kiss album – so loose, in fact, that Peter Criss makes a joke about marshmallows as the tape starts to roll.

■ 100,000 Years

A demo track recorded at New York's Bell Sound studios just before Kiss cut their first album.

■ Stop, Look To Listen

A Paul Stanley song that was recorded in 1966 when he and his friends Matt Rael and Neil Teeman (guitarist and drummer respectively) were just 14! The song was recorded at New York's Mayfair studios, where Teeman worked as a part-time cleaner. The song features no bass guitar simply because none of the three friends could play bass. The style is typical mid 60s rock redolent of The Who and The Kinks.

■ Leeta

Written by Gene Simmons in 1969 when he was a member of a smalltime band called Bullfrog Bheer, "Leeta" is a one-take recording that was cut at New York's Sanders studios. Simmons is backed by Bullfrog Bheer on this weepie, inspired by the harmony sound of the Everly Brothers.

■ Let Me Go, Rock'n'Roll

Another 1973 demo from the same Bell Sound sessions as "100,000 Years", notable for Simmons' jokey ad-libs and a belch at the beginning.

■ Acrobat

Written by Simmons and Frehley, this song would be reworked as a shortened instrumental for the first Kiss album under the new title of "Love Theme From Kiss". This version was recorded live at The Daisy in Long Island, New York, on August 25, 1973.

Fire House

A demo recording from the Bell Sound sessions, which features a false start and general in-the-studio tom-foolery.

Doncha Hesitate

Written by Paul Stanley in 1975 after the huge success of *Alive!*, this carefree rocker is more in tune with earlier albums like *Dressed To Kill* and so was rejected for the group's next album, *Destroyer*. Recorded at Magna Graphic studios in New York's fashionable Greenwich Village.

Mad Dog

A Gene Simmons tune demo'ed for *Destroyer* but reworked as the core riff to that album's "Flaming Youth" track.

God Of Thunder

The original version of the song features writer Paul Stanley singing lead. This version is sleeker and faster than the *Destroyer* recording and was cut by Simmons and Stanley with Kiss tour manager J R Smalling playing drums. Stanley says he was "floored" when *Destroyer* producer Bob Ezrin suggested that Simmons sing the song!

Bad, Bad Lovin'

This Gene Simmons song, written one afternoon in 1976, was later reshaped into "Calling Dr. Love" for the *Rock And Roll Over* album.

Mr. Speed

A demo from *Rock And Roll Over*, featuring Bob Kulick on guitar. Drummer unknown.

I Want You

Recorded during a soundcheck at the Los Angeles Forum in August 1977.

Love Gun

An amazingly high-quality demo of one of Paul Stanley's greatest songs. Paul plays all instruments apart from drums, which are played by Steve Korff of New York band The Planets.

Love Is Blind

An acoustic tune written and recorded by Gene Simmons after a Kiss gig in 1977. The vocal harmonies are reminiscent of the Eagles and the bass riff echoes Otis Redding's soul standard "(Sittin' On) The Dock Of The Bay".

Radioactive

A demo version of the song from Gene Simmons' solo album. Simmons's original intention was for rock'n'roll legend Jerry Lee Lewis to record the song on an album Simmons would produce, but Kiss manager Bill Aucoin rejected the idea.

You're All That I Want, You're All That I Need

A demo of the song which featured on the *Unmasked* album as simply "You're All That I Want". Recorded in 1977 and originally slated for the *Love Gun* album.

Talk To Me

A live recording from Kiss's record-breaking Australian tour of 1980, performed to 60,000 fans at Sydney's Parreta Stadium.

Time Traveller

A demo recorded in 1986 at Paul Stanley's New York apartment. The song was written by Stanley and Desmond Child for the *Crazy Nights* album, but did not make the cut. It combines the commercial rock sound of *Crazy Nights* with the pomp of *The Elder*.

Ain't That Peculiar

An Eric Carr song which later formed the basis for "Little Caesar", from the *Hot In The Shade* album.

Domino

A demo of the song from the *Revenge* album, recorded with members of Silent Rage, who were signed to Gene Simmons' label Simmons Records.

Nothing Can Keep Me From You

Written by Diane Warren for the soundtrack to the

Gene Simmons: "Thank you – good night!"

Ace and Paul meet the fans

Kiss-inspired movie *Detroit Rock City*. A power ballad sung by Paul Stanley.

■ It's My Life

A Simmons/Stanley track recorded by Kiss for the *Psycho Circus* album and originally recorded by Wendy O. Williams, the outrageous former singer for US shock rockers The Plasmatics. Williams was famed for chainsawing cars in half onstage and appearing topless save for gaffa tape over her nipples. She committed suicide in the late 1990s.

■ Rock And Roll All Nite

A taster for the *Alive IV* album, Kiss's greatest anthem as recorded on Millennium Eve 1999 at the BC Place Stadium in Vancouver, Canada.

DISCOGRAPHY

Kiss, 1974

Hotter Than Hell, 1974

Dressed To Kill, 1975

Alive!, 1975

Destroyer, 1976

Rock And Roll Over, 1976

Love Gun, 1977

Alive II, 1977

Double Platinum, 1978

Gene Simmons, 1978

Paul Stanley, 1978

Ace Frehley, 1978

Peter Criss, 1978

Dynasty, 1979

Unmasked, 1980

The Elder, 1981

Killers, 1982

Creatures Of The Night, 1982

Lick It Up, 1983

Animalize, 1984

Asylum, 1985

Crazy Nights, 1987

Smashes, Thrashes & Hits, 1988

Hot In The Shade, 1989

Revenge, 1992

Alive III, 1993

Unplugged, 1996

You Wanted The Best, 1996

Greatest Kiss, 1997

Carnival Of Souls, 1997

Psycho Circus, 1998

Box Set, 2001

INDEX